# Accounting Services, Growth, and Change in the Pacific Basin

# ACCOUNTING SERVICES, GROWTH, AND CHANGE IN THE PACIFIC BASIN

DAVID L. McKEE

DON E. GARNER

**QUORUM BOOKS**
Westport, Connecticut • London

**Library of Congress Cataloging-in-Publication Data**

McKee, David L.
    Accounting services, growth, and change in the Pacific Basin /
    David L. McKee, Don E. Garner.
       p.  cm.
    Includes bibliographical references and index.
    ISBN 1–56720–017–6 (alk. paper)
    1. Accounting firms—Asia, Southeastern.  2. Accounting firms—
    East Asia.  3. Accounting firms—Pacific Area.  I. Garner, Don E.,
    II. Title.
    HF5616.A785M36   1996
    338.7′61657′099—dc20      95–37480

British Library Cataloguing in Publication Data is available.

Library of Congress Catalog Card Number: 95–37480
ISBN: 1–56720–017–6

First published in 1996

Quorum Books, 88 Post Road West, Westport, CT 06881
An imprint of Greenwood Publishing Group, Inc.

Printed in the United States of America

The paper used in this book complies with the
Permanent Paper Standard issued by the National
Information Standards Organization (Z39.48–1984).

10 9 8 7 6 5 4 3 2 1

# CONTENTS

# Acknowledgments

This project could not have been completed without the editorial assistance of Linda Poje, who prepared the typescript and assisted in all phases of manuscript preparation. Special thanks are also extended to Constantin Ogloblin, who assembled the index and also to Kenneth Toursounov.

# INTRODUCTION

The second half of the twentieth century has been characterized by the emergence of a truly global economy. The ending of the Cold War has added an extra impetus to the ongoing expansion of that economy by creating larger global markets as well as by downsizing military demands on resource pools. Nowhere has the potential of new international markets seemed more compelling than in the region of the world known as the Pacific Basin. Indeed, in some circles the approaching twenty-first century is being heralded as the Pacific Century. Whether such a prophecy is overly optimistic remains to be seen.

No one disputes the role that advances in transportation and communications have played in the emergence of the global economy. Indeed, without such advances there would be much less to discuss with respect to the economic and business potential of the Pacific Basin. In addition, various cadres of services have emerged as facilitators of business activity and economic linkages in the international economy.

This book acknowledges the role played by producer services in general and speaks of those offered by the major accounting firms in particular upon the growth prospects for various Pacific Basin nations. The jurisdictions considered are divided into three subgroups. The first group comprises the four newly industrialized nations that have become known as the Asian Tigers: Hong Kong, Singapore, Taiwan and South Korea. The second group is composed of emerging nations—Indonesia, Malaysia, the Philippines and Thailand. The final group is made up of a selection of small island states.

In choosing such a set of groupings the intent was to show both the real and the potential impacts of the accounting firms in varying circumstances. The book will review the impact of the accounting firms in nations of various sizes and levels of material strength. It will speak as well to the international linkage functions that firms perform.

In pursuing this agenda, the authors have divided the volume into four major sections. Part I sets the general frame of reference for the discussion. It begins with some general observations concerning the role of services in the Pacific region. Following that, international linkages as they pertain to various Pacific economies are discussed. The section closes with a discussion of the role of accounting services in economic expansion.

In Part II of the volume the emphasis switches to a description of the institutional parameters for accounting practice. In this section the domestic business and legal environments facing accounting practice are reviewed, as are the scope and operating rules of the accounting profession. This section sets the stage for understanding the climate facing the major international accounting firms as they endeavor to service the needs of their clients in the various national groupings that are being discussed.

Part III switches the emphasis to developmental concerns among the national groupings selected and to the real and potential contributions of the international accounting firms. In this section, separate chapters assess the economic impact of the firms in nations within the three subgroupings alluded to earlier.

The final section of the book (Part IV) reviews the institutional climate in the national subgroups and assesses the potential for growth and change among them, as influenced by the accounting firms. In this section the diverse elements of the project are pulled together with an eye to sorting out the policy implications of what the firms are doing. By combining economic and accounting expertise, it is hoped that the book will provide a better understanding of the problems of change as they impact business operations among the nation groups that are reviewed. It is also hoped that the book will provide some insights with respect to the potential role of the firms in facilitating the kinds of international linkages that most of the nations reviewed appear to require as a foundation for their economic improvement.

# PART I

## THE GENERAL FRAME OF REFERENCE

# I

# Some Preliminary Observations Concerning Services

In an area as large and diverse as the Pacific Basin it seems clear that the level of economic intercourse that exists at present could hardly have been achieved without the advances in transportation and communications that have been characteristic of the second half of the twentieth century. Indeed, those basic service categories have been joined by various other service pursuits in facilitating the emergence of a truly global economy. The roles of the nations of the Pacific in that economy have been impacted by the services in question, as has the development of the domestic economies of those nations. Clearly, services are fulfilling both domestic and international functions in the Pacific Basin.

Service expansion in that arena is simultaneously a causal element in the growth of various domestic economies and the linkages that have been being forged between them and a result or effect of the needs of specific economies, whether domestic or external. In the present context the traditional discussions of services as they relate to urban expansion or growth in income will not suffice. Few would dispute the role that urbanization has played in service expansion in advanced economies. The case of income as a stimulus to service expansion may be somewhat more difficult to endorse in its most general form, but certainly the demand for certain services would appear to be income elastic.

Within the context of the Pacific Basin an understanding of service roles must go beyond what has been stated above. Services of various types have become important components of the economies of both advanced and emerging nations. Their importance appears to be on the rise in most jurisdictions, despite wide variations in cultures. The level of development appears to be a poor benchmark for measuring their importance, as various services are expanding in both advanced and emerging nations.

Some services may have actual roles in the development process (McKee 1988; McKee and Garner 1992). They act as facilitators of economic activity within nations at various levels of development. Others carry their facilitative impacts beyond national boundaries into the world economy. As has been emphasized elsewhere, however, "Services cannot be regarded as mere facilitators in the international economy" (McKee and Garner 1992). As important as the facilitative functions of services may be, it must be remembered that those same services "are actually being traded in that economy and in many instances have become internationalized in their own right" (1992). These considerations must be dealt with if any real understanding of service roles or impacts in the Pacific Basin is to be achieved.

Advanced economies in the Pacific theater have been the locus of development for various sophisticated service groupings that have used such locations to extend their impacts both internationally and, more specifically, to less-developed economies. The penetration of specific Third World jurisdictions by services from abroad is no doubt dictated by the desire of the firms in question to remain competitive in the processes of satisfying the actual or anticipated needs of their customers. As many of those customers are multinational firms, it is hardly surprising that various sophisticated business services are cropping up in areas of the Pacific that are hosting production facilities geared to international markets. The specific impacts of services in such jurisdictions will depend upon how well they serve their clients and of course upon their potential for impacting domestic host economies directly.

It has been suggested with respect to the international economy that as U.S. service firms expanded they "played a key role in many countries in creating a domestic market" (Noyelle and Dutka 1988, 29). In doing so they were often filling a vacuum caused by the lack of experienced domestic firms (1988, 29). The expansion of producer services and hence the rising impact of services has been attributed to various causes. Writing in 1989, Peter Enderwick cited what he considered to be three principal factors. First of all, he suggested, "the extension of the inter-industry division of labour has resulted in the expansion of industries such as distribution, banking, insurance and finance serving the needs of material producers" (1989, 6). Certainly accounting and various international legal services, not to mention various highly specialized consulting activities, could be added to the list without altering the direction of Enderwick's analysis. Second among his factors underlying the expansion of producer services were "occupations such as technologists and managers" (6). These categories "have grown as organizations pursuing geographical and industrial diversification have faced increasingly complex problems of administration and control" (6). As the final causal element behind the growth of producer services, Enderwick saw the increasing importance of product differentiation. He saw differentiation as based more and more "on the conjunction of material and non-material goods" or, in other words, complementarity between goods and service functions (6–7).

If Enderwick's perceptions are accurate, the service expansion visible in the Pacific Basin hardly seems to be surprising. The international linkages that appear to have been forged there have created a fertile climate for continuing service expansion. At the same time it must be remembered that various service categories themselves have made fundamental contributions to the existing linkages. Thus the Pacific Basin appears to provide a very good laboratory for examining both the domestic and international roles of services.

Enderwick's view of services in the international sphere goes well beyond a mere endorsement of facilitator roles. In a recent study of services in a developmental context, he suggested that the enabling role for services understates their importance (1991, 294). "This is because services are typically characterized by significant economic linkages and the generation of externalities" (294). He sees such linkages as externalities in transportation services and, in the case of the labor force, as benefits to be had from education and health services (294).

Beyond what has been cited above, Enderwick sees linkage effects and positive externalities in the provision of various producer services such as insurance and finance. Both of those service categories, he argues, act in various ways to strengthen the economies within which they operate. Specifically, he argues with respect to insurance that "the pooling of risks and premiums provides not only a widening and deepening of financial markets but additionally a stimulus to saving, credit facilitation and the promotion of new economic activities" (294). Of course various services that affect business will generate positive externalities and linkages. Accounting services, for example, have been identified as a source of various linkage effects (McKee and Garner 1992).

In the case of accounting services the linkage effects have often been the result of the operations of large international accounting firms. Enderwick would hardly be surprised at what has been occurring in the case of accounting services in the world economy. He sees a potential for the development of multinational service activities in emerging nations, which would presumably become major players impacting development. A role for services in Third World developmental processes has been recognized (McKee 1988), but no comprehensive treatment of the myriad of service subsectors as they relate to economic expansion is readily available.

The importance of services in the economies of advanced nations is no longer debated. Their significance in various Third World jurisdictions is at least suggested. They are recognized as playing a significant and increasing role in the international economy. Despite this seemingly universal recognition of their importance, difficulties still remain with respect to accounting for them in trade between nations and indeed even in measuring the productivity of specific services in the economies that house them.

The emphasis in the pursuit of an understanding of services may have switched from discussions with respect to productivity to more specific interests in service functions and impacts. Despite this, doubts concerning the present and future prospects of economies that are placing too much emphasis on services or where services are expanding rapidly seem to linger. Services may still be thought of as a residual category or a set of pursuits adopted as next best by defaulting manufacturing economies.

The presumption of weaknesses in manufacturing as a causal element in service expansion is an oversimplification. It has been suggested that "the share of employment in the production of goods for all high income economies will eventually become so small as to be negligible" (Cooper 1988, 250). Cooper went on to suggest that, in the case of the United States, "allowing for those employees who are really engaged in the production of services rather than the production of goods, total goods production today [1988] is undertaken with less than ten percent of the labour force" (1988, 250). Cooper proclaimed the production worker to be a disappearing breed, while acknowledging that "the rate of his disappearance will vary from country to country" (250). His analysis does not identify him as a subscriber to the belief in an existing or impending industrial debacle. He is merely referring to declining labor requirements in manufacturing processes. In the face of that, the actual state of the service sector would require further analysis.

Economies that have become service oriented, as judged by the percentages of their labor forces employed in such pursuits, can hardly be categorized as being beyond their prime. In economies where as little as 10 percent of employment opportunities reside in actual production processes, the service sector can hardly be considered to be a residual category, much less a fallback destination for surplus labor. Earlier in the history of those economies, when employment in manufacturing pursuits, most particularly assembly-line operations, was expanding, agricultural productivity was improving, thus necessitating fewer farm workers. Few economists saw these parallel circumstances as signalling the impending demise of economies that had been based historically on agriculture. Indeed, some economic historians have suggested that economies move through a progression from agriculture to manufacturing to services. Without joining the never-ending debate concerning stage theories, suffice it to say that economies require a mix of the outputs of all three sectors (Amara 1993a).

The ascendancy of manufacturing need not signal the demise of agriculture or other primary pursuits. Similarly, service expansion is neither a cause nor an effect of declines in manufacturing activities. It is possible in some cases for economies to move beyond primary pursuits into services without any intermediate flirtation with manufacturing (Amara 1993b). In many cases, economies that are modernizing may find both improvements in agricultural productivity and the expansion of manufacturing and service pursuits occurring within the same time frame. Clearly, service growth in any national economy, not to mention the international sphere, is a rather complicated phenomenon that must be examined in its own right, free from judgmental preconceptions, if its true implications are to be understood.

For the pursuit of the objective referred to above, the Pacific Basin appears to afford a reasonable theater of operations. It is advantageous in that regard not because it constitutes an international economy in its own right but because of the diversity of domestic economies it embraces and because of the expanded intercourse among those economies that the service revolution has generated. It has been only through considerable service inputs that the trans-Pacific trading linkages of the 1990s have emerged.

Of course, economies in and around the Pacific Basin were involved in international trading activities long before the revolution in transportation and communications that has lumped them together as subjects for investigation. European nations such as France and Great Britain had long-standing colonial and commercial interests in Southeast Asia. The United States has had interests in the Pacific throughout most of its history. Other European nations were also involved in the Pacific—Spain in the Philippines and the Dutch in Indonesia. The islands of the South Pacific were also linked to various developed nations, although those relationships for the most part were products of the late nineteenth century (McKee and Tisdell 1990).

The types of relationships listed above were hardly responsible for the emergence of the Pacific Ocean as a unifying element among the nations surrounding it. Historically the Pacific has posed a serious barrier to international linkages. It has been only in the second half of the twentieth century that the technologies of linkage have encouraged the steadily expanding economic interactions that have attracted the interests of economists and others concerned with international business. With these changes have come the emergence of Japan as a world economic power and the success of outward-looking developmental strategies among various Asian nations. Newly industrialized economies such as Hong Kong, Korea, Singapore and Taiwan have made notable strides in strengthening themselves through manufacturing for export. Known as the Asian Tigers, those economies have recently been joined by Thailand, which appears to have become successful in following a similar path.

There is little doubt that such strategies have increased economic linkages in the Pacific Basin. With the dismantling of the British Empire in the post-World War II era, various jurisdictions were forced to move beyond their former colonial linkages. As the United Kingdom moved more and more toward the European orbit, even such nations as Australia, Canada and New Zealand were forced to adjust their trading patterns.

The geopolitical concerns of the United States have also affected growth patterns in various Pacific jurisdictions. There is little doubt of this influence in the case of nations like South Korea, the Philippines and Taiwan. It may also be true in the case of Japan. During the period of the Cold War, not only was the United States careful to maintain a military presence in the Pacific, it also sought to encourage the emergence of strong profit-motivated economies as a counterweight to possible communist expansion.

In some cases geopolitical considerations appear to have hastened the transfer of technology. This may have occurred somewhat in various manufacturing industries but more importantly in transportation and communications infrastructures. It was of course the emergence of such infrastructures that made the United States a more viable market for manufactured goods from the Far East. Geopolitical concerns may have also contributed to the opening up of this market. While insuring cooperation from various nations in guarding against possible communist expansion, it was natural for the United States to entertain trading relationships.

Thus, linkages of an economic character have emerged between the United States and various Far Eastern nations. At the same time Australia and New Zealand have been developing trading relations in the Pacific theater as their economic ties to the United Kingdom have been receding.

Those same nations have gradually developed more linkages to the small island jurisdictions in the Pacific. The United States also assumed more economic responsibilities in various island territories in the aftermath of World War II. All of the linkages referred to in this paragraph have been assisted and emphasized by the emergence of various international services.

The importance of services to the development and facilitation of economic activity in the Pacific Basin can be seen in the emergence of service centers designed to supply the needs of international business. Notable among those have been Hong Kong and Singapore. Various South Pacific island jurisdictions have been attempting to assume the role of offshore service centers, with relatively modest results at this writing. That economic forces in the United States economy are responding to the pull of the Pacific can be seen in the emergence of San Francisco as a locus for business-oriented services aimed at the international economy or, more notably, the needs of the Pacific theater. The importance of services can be seen as well in the way in which the economy of Hawaii has developed. This is especially true of the Honolulu area, which has developed a service base well beyond the traditional and expanding needs of the tourist industry.

Although components of Hong Kong's manufacturing sector have been shifting their locations to adjacent territories of mainland China, the inexorable movement of the colony toward 1997 may be actually enhancing its functions as a trading and service center. Despite the shift of various activities from Hong Kong to Singapore and even to Vancouver, the colony's role as a transshipment center and entrepôt may actually be enhanced by its entry into the economy of China. There is little doubt that China will require a window on the world and a point of access to the international economy. Hong Kong, with its international service tradition, seems well suited to those responsibilities. Whether it will retain its present functions and move even further in the direction cited here must await the transition that 1997 will bring. Should Hong Kong stumble in the transition, for whatever reasons, other jurisdictions will be available to take up the slack.

The Far East has already developed a major service center in the form of Tokyo. The Japanese metropolis has been recognized as being on a par with London and New York as a global service center (Sassen 1991). Certainly the emergence of such a complex contributes to the trans-Pacific linkages that have been referred to. In Australia and New Zealand, Sydney and Aukland have emerged as major players in the supplying of international services. The positioning of service metropoles such as those alluded to in this chapter have contributed to regional, transoceanic and in some cases global linkages. They have certainly been instrumental in setting trading patterns in the Pacific Basin and also in establishing the development potential of various jurisdictions.

Considering the size of the area it would be an overstatement to suggest that the Pacific Basin is ringed by international service metropoles that have drawn it together into a tightly integrated trading region. Despite some penetration of Latin American markets by the Japanese, most of the Hispanic nations fronting on the Pacific still look to the United States or to Europe with respect to extraregional trading linkages. The transportation and communications infrastructures, not to mention other business-related service support systems, aimed at bridging the Pacific have not emerged. Whether the future holds such developments remains to be seen.

Service metropoles could certainly be regarded as growth centers in the sense that the term has come to be used by many economists. Essentially they represent real-world manifestations of the spatial positioning of forces that influence economic change both domestically and internationally. This view of service metropoles can probably trace its patrimony to an explanation of economic change known as *pole theory*. No doubt Francois Perroux and other early pole theorists might not have subscribed to such an overt geographical emphasis. Nonetheless, the often-quoted declaration that "growth does not appear everywhere at the same time, it becomes manifest at points or poles of growth, with variable intensity, it spreads through different channels, with variable terminal effects on the whole of the economy" (Perroux 1970, 94) seems to apply.

Even though Perroux was speaking abstractly of firms or industries as the focus of uneven growth and even though he and other pole theorists saw such firms or industries in leadership roles as instruments of change, it seems as though the service metropoles alluded to above may themselves be central to the growth and change that seem to be occurring in the Pacific Basin. Perroux once described space as a field of forces, as centers or poles "from which centrifugal forces emanate and to which centripetal forces are attracted" (1950).

It may appear to be too large a leap to suggest that the various service metropoles listed above, or others unnamed, are actual growth poles in the Pacific Basin. Examples of service industries that are growth poles are relatively rare. Nonetheless, "Most pole theorists today have accepted the notion of growth centers" (McKee 1988, 18). By doing so they are probably not endorsing the notion of service growth poles but appear rather to be recognizing urban settings as climates well suited for industrial activity. In a sense they are using climate in a Schumpeterian context (McKee 1991).

If the metropoles of the Pacific are harboring leading industrial activities, they could undoubtedly be defined as growth centers or as places "from which centrifugal forces emanate and to which centripetal forces are attracted" (Perroux 1950).

Of course the force field concept, as seen by Perroux, was an abstraction that seemed to explain industries or perhaps firms rather than places per se. This can be seen in another view of space that he subscribed to. In this view he referred to "the set of relationships which exist between the firm and, on the one hand, the suppliers of input . . . and, on the other hand, the buyers of output (both intermediate and final)" (1950). It must be remembered that the pole theorists and Perroux in particular saw growth and change as a dialectic process whereby the leading sectors of an economy are replaced over time by new aspirants to leadership. The changes in leadership were seen as occurring through innovative processes in particular industries that pushed their hosts to the forefront.

Neither Perroux nor Schumpeter before him was especially concerned with service activities as focal points for change. Yet in the Pacific Basin innovations in a wide variety of services related to production have been very visible in the processes of change. The grouping of those activities in various metropoles has contributed to preserving climates conducive to production. In such settings they have undoubtedly supported the growth of domestic economies, and beyond that they have facilitated international trade. In this context they are taking part both in building and supporting international relationships between firms and the suppliers of resource inputs and in the supply or delivery of final outputs to consumers, whether corporations, governments or individuals.

They perform such functions both domestically and internationally, and in the latter case they are actually internationalizing economic space and indeed contributing to the development of force fields of the sort envisaged by Perroux. In all of this, however, they are more than facilitators, for they are either being traded themselves or expanding into new locations as branches of multinational service firms. Thus, they are not simply internationalizing economic space, they have become an integral part of it.

Enderwick was correct in recognizing the complementarity that has arisen between manufacturing and services (1989, 6–7). It is recognized that certain business-related services position themselves internationally to meet the needs of the production units of multinational firms (McKee and Garner 1992). This pattern of expansion is in evidence in the Pacific Basin. It certainly signals a form of complementarity between production units and specific services. However, service purveyors may proliferate internationally to remain competitive with rivals that are doing so. The complementarity of specific services to specific production units may be somewhat less binding than in textbook examples of complementarity. Specific services hardly relate to specific production facilities as neckties to shirts.

Of course, successful relationships between services and manufacturing firms result in products in which the service content is far from obvious. Whether the services were supplied by specialized staffs within manufacturing firms or purchased from profit-seeking independent service firms, the success of the services results in a product in which they cannot be recognized. Elsewhere, services in the industrial sector have been described as " 'always a bridesmaid, never a bride'—they perform an important function in the manufacturing process, but they are never present at its consummation,—the final utilization of its output" (McKee 1988, 20). They are rarely purchased by the consumers of products as are shirts and neckties.

If business services are to meet the needs of specific manufacturing endeavors, then the success (profitability) of the services in question over time might be thought to depend upon the continued success of their clients. Presumably, services in various locations in the Pacific Basin owe their success to being able to satisfy industrial clients that are themselves enjoying continuing success. Although this is true, the type of complementarity that exists in such cases can hardly be considered to be a shirt-and-necktie situation. Should specific manufacturing activities fall upon hard times, it is hardly predetermined that the services that have been linked to them will decline in consort.

Services are not, generally speaking, industry- or firm-specific. When firms or industries go into decline or lose their leadership positions, business-related services contribute to maintaining a climate conducive to the emergence of new industrial leaders. Thus, they aid in supporting growth and change and in preventing secular declines. In this respect they have roles that are far more important than what might be presumed for complements to specific industrial processes. They may prolong the life of such processes in certain settings, while also facilitating growth and change on both domestic and international levels. It is in this respect that they appear to be major contributors to expanding economic activity throughout the Pacific Basin. Unfortunately, general data concerning their operations are very difficult to attain. A better understanding of their nature and the extent of their impact will probably have to await a careful compilation of information on a service-by-service basis. Beyond that, information on each service will have to be attained for every individual jurisdiction concerned.

Only then will the impact of services in an area as large and diverse as the Pacific Basin be adequately understood.

# 2

# INTERNATIONAL LINKAGES AND EMERGING ECONOMIES IN THE PACIFIC

In the second half of the twentieth century the Pacific Basin has emerged as an area perceived as having great economic and business potential. Indeed, some students of the global economy are already labeling the year 2000 as the dawn of the Pacific Century. Without such an extravagant endorsement it seems safe to suggest that many Pacific nations are already increasing their involvement in the international economy and that the immediate future holds the promise of increased trans-Pacific business and economic ties. The presumed accuracy of such observations hardly justifies regarding the Pacific or, more accurately, the nations that are in it or near it as an emerging economic region or distinct subset of the global economy.

## HISTORICAL BACKGROUND

Anyone who has ever crossed the Pacific Ocean will recognize it as a barrier rather than a unifying force in the world economy. It was a desire on the part of European nations for a shorter route to the Far East that led to the voyages of discovery and ultimately to interest in the Americas. Even after the Western Hemisphere had been settled and the Pacific circumnavigated, the New World was hardly regarded by Europeans as a jumping-off spot for commerce with the Far East. It has been advances in transportation and communications in the second half of the twentieth-century that have heightened economic and business interest in Asia and the Pacific Basin on the part of Canada and the United States, not to mention interest in North American markets on the part of various Far Eastern nations.

Traditionally the Pacific has been a barrier to economic and business interests. The commerce between Europe and Asia that prompted the voyages of discovery was hardly heightened by the circumnavigation of the globe. The first British settlements in Australia emerged little more than two hundred years ago. Initially Australia was regarded as a dumping ground for felons and indigents rather than a source of wealth. The islands of the South Pacific received little interest on the part of the colonial powers until late in the nineteenth century. Japan had been able to resist contact with the West until the middle of that century. The opening of the Panama Canal was a stimulus to better linkages between the western coast of North America and Europe rather than a shortcut between Europe and the Far East.

The commerce between Europe and Asia began with overland routes and expanded by sea around Africa and across the Indian Ocean. Various European colonial powers acquired stakes in Asia and the Far East, but the Pacific Ocean had little to do with those occurrences. It seems clear that economic interest in the Pacific would have been even slower in emerging in the absence of major markets and economic players in North America.

In a historical sense interest in the Pacific on the part of the United States was largely geopolitical. That nation's control over the Philippines stemmed from the Spanish-American War. As Japan emerged as a military power in the period leading up to World War II, the United States based substantial military resources in Hawaii. Of course, in that period isolationist sentiment was strong in the United States, and the deployment of military forces in Hawaii was hardly an effort to assert any absolute control in the Pacific. Instead, it was a visible statement of strength, a forward observation post from which to monitor unfolding events and a defensive position designed to discourage military ambitions that might threaten the Hawaiian Islands themselves and areas of the Pacific closer to the North American mainland.

Suffice it to say that the attack on Pearl Harbor and the subsequent involvement of the United States in World War II permanently altered that nation's involvement in the Pacific. Aside from maintaining a postwar presence in the Far East, the United States assumed an active military role in the Pacific. Events involving China and Taiwan, the Korean War and of course Vietnam, not to mention mutual defense initiatives, made the United States a major player in the Pacific Basin. As the American presence became stronger, European interest in the Asian theater of geopolitical operations was on the wane.

The rebuilding of the Japanese economy in a peacetime industrial mold and the gradual emergence of export-oriented manufacturing sectors in Hong Kong, Singapore, South Korea and Taiwan increased the potential for economic and commercial contacts between the United States and the Far East. Of course, such contacts were facilitated by advances in transportation and communications.

Japan, followed by the four other jurisdictions listed above, became interested in doing business with the United States because of the size of that nation's domestic markets. The United States in turn has been showing increasing interest in the huge potential market for goods and services that the Far East represents. Thus interests on both sides of the Pacific are encouraging trade across a barrier grown smaller in recent years. Such interests are hardly turning the Pacific Basin into a region, nor are they bridging the cultural gaps among among the peoples of the various nations concerned. In the Pacific the interests in question are pressing the nations concerned into seemingly ever-increasing participatory positions within the world economy.

Aside from cultural and ethnic diversity, the nations of the Pacific Basin encompass major differences in economic strength and growth potential. They range from global economic powers such as Japan and the United States to the island ministates of the South Pacific, many of which are severely constrained in terms of economic potential. They encompass the relatively wealthy nations of Canada, Australia and New Zealand as well as the newly industrialized nations referred to earlier in the present chapter. Island nations such as Indonesia and the Philippines present economic circumstances far different from those of other jurisdictions mentioned in this paragraph. In short, the nations of the Pacific Basin are facing a wide variety of economic circumstances.

Any understanding of economic events involving the Pacific Basin rests upon an understanding of the various nations and cultures concerned. Among those nations, regional subgroups have certain economic strengths and weaknesses in common. It is legitimate to ask how the fortunes of such jurisdictions may be impacted by improved transportation and communications or any other linking factors that may shrink the Pacific as an obstacle or provide new transoceanic opportunities. Clearly, the answer to such a question will depend upon the size, strength and positioning of the individual jurisdictions concerned.

## SMALL ISLAND STATES

Among the jurisdictions most heavily impacted by their position in the Pacific Basin are the small island states that dot the ocean. Economists have recognized that small economies are by and large far more dependent upon foreign trade than are larger jurisdictions (Smith 1987; McKee and Tisdell 1990; Abu Amara 1991). Smith attributes this to the probability that smaller economies have a narrower range of resources, "which encourages concentration on a few traded goods industries, and because foreign trade is the only means by which small countries can benefit from efficiency gains that scale production can allow in even a few product lines" (1987, 239). Because of the size of domestic markets, most small economies must place heavy reliance upon external sources for most manufactured or processed goods. In other words, the accoutrements of modern lifestyles can only be acquired internationally.

Smith attests to a heavy reliance on foreign trade on the part of South Pacific island countries (239). In that regard he adds that various island economies are dependent upon very limited exports to a small number of markets (239). Traditionally distance has added to the developmental impediments that the island ministates of the South Pacific have faced. Whether recent improvements in transportation and communications make the prognosis for those jurisdictions more optimistic must be dealt with on a case-by-case basis.

Certainly, distance from suppliers has raised the costs of imports. On the other side of the ledger the attractiveness of exports from the ministates in question has hardly been enhanced by their locations. These islands form three main groupings: "Micronesia encompasses the area mainly north of the equator and west of the dateline. Melanesia covers the region south of the equator and west of the dateline. The third subregion is known as Polynesia" (McKee and Tisdell 1990, x). Although Europeans did establish plantations in all three regions, these linkages were relatively late in coming "and in many Pacific countries traditional subsistence activity remained dominant" (6). By and large, with the exception of French holdings, colonial control lasted for less than 100 years, and continuing linkages with European powers were less strong than has been the case in other parts of the world, notably the Caribbean.

In the latter half of the nineteenth century, partially because of growing intercourse between Western nations and China and Japan, "the region became more integrated with the main international trade routes" (Browne 1989, 1). According to Browne, Europe and North America drew upon the region for foodstuffs and coconut products that furnished soap and edible oils (1). Foreigners acquired land for plantations in Fiji, Solomon Islands, Papua New Guinea and Western Samoa (1), among other locations. "Mining operations commenced in a few islands, including the extraction of gold on Papua New Guinea and phosphate in Kiribati" (2).

As many of the island economies gained their political independence in the second half of the twentieth century, their economies were still dominated by agriculture. This was hardly a solid basis for improving their economic circumstances, given that the terms of trade had turned against primary commodities (Nurkse 1967). Nonetheless, as Browne has suggested, plantations dating from the nineteenth century were still in operation under foreign management in several jurisdictions (1989, 3). As is known to economists, staple enterprises are often not designed with the needs of host jurisdictions in mind (McKee and Tisdell 1990, 5).

"In small island economies . . . the continuing reliance on staple exports may preclude the development of inter island intercourse" (10). Poor or worsening terms of trade may put pressure on such jurisdictions to increase primary exports in hopes of earning the foreign exchange needed for imports that are becoming relatively more expensive. This pattern places small island states such as those under discussion in competition with each other, which in turn may preclude productive interisland relationships. As has been recognized, these circumstances may well block collective efforts on the part of island groups to practice import substitution (10).

As domestic markets are generally small in the jurisdictions under discussion, it is hardly surprising that manufacturing activities aimed at such markets have been slow to emerge. Of course, the lack of a basis for cooperation between nations in developing such enterprises has contributed to that slow emergence. Manufacturing development varies widely throughout the region. It was seen to be most pronounced in Fiji and New Guinea and developed to a lesser extent in Western Samoa (Fairbairn and Parry 1986, 26). However, even in those countries it was seen as contributing less than 10 percent to gross domestic product (27).

Browne cites Fiji as having a larger manufacturing sector than the other island economies (1989, 9). He sees opportunities for export-oriented production as having been enhanced "by the provision, since 1981, of duty free access to the Australian and New Zealand markets under a South Pacific regional trade agreement" (9). Australian investment has aided manufacturing in Fiji (Fairbairn and Parry 1986, 27). "Several industrial ventures have been established . . . mostly in the area of import substitution, which includes the manufacture of copra oil, canned fish, beer, cigarettes, biscuits, paint, plastic products, light engineering products, and wood products" (27).

Fairbairn and Parry noted that foreign participation in manufacturing in various Pacific island nations was limited and was virtually absent in very small countries (27). However, they suggested that multinational corporations could expand export-oriented production, citing new export opportunities involving Australia and New Zealand (28). Of course, those two nations were among the most likely trading partners for many of the islands in question.

Whether or not recent improvements in transportation and communications will broaden export markets for the islands of the South Pacific remains to be seen. There is certainly room for skepticism. The islands in question "do not offer wage advantages over Southeast Asian countries, such as the Philippines" (McKee and Tisdell 1990, 20). In addition "supporting services for manufacturing, including regular shipment possibilities, are less developed" (20). It seems reasonable to presume that multinational firms seeking low wage-cost locations in the Pacific are likely to prefer Southeast Asian locations over the small island nations.

Fairbairn and Parry suggested that multinational firms in the service sector have been significant in the South Pacific. Such firms "have provided importing, wholesaling, and retailing activities, as well as banking, financing, and other services" (18). In South Pacific ministates, "The names of leading . . . trading houses are household words, and through fairly aggressive promotional advertising they continue to exert a disproportionate influence on the behavior of Pacific island consumers" (28). If Fairbairn and Parry were accurate in their observations, it may be that various services that are international in nature may find productive involvements in the island economies under consideration. Such involvements will undoubtedly impact development potential in states where they occur. At the very least they should strengthen the international linkages of the nations in question.

## NEWLY INDUSTRIALIZED ECONOMIES

If the economic future of the ministates of the South Pacific seems somewhat tenuous, more optimistic forecasts can be applied to various other nations sharing exposure to the Pacific Basin. In 1991, *The Economist* declared that "The four economic 'Tigers' of East Asia—South Korea, Taiwan, Singapore and Hong Kong—have forged the fastest industrial revolution the world has ever seen" (*The Economist* Supplement 1991, 3). The four nations in question have been leading exponents of a growth strategy based upon manufacturing for export. Although there is room for discussion with respect to how they have fared in terms of domestic development, few economists appear ready to dispute their growth records. They "have been among the most spectacular performers in the world economy over the past 25 years, quadrupling their shares of world production and trade" (Noland 1990, 15).

Although widely used, the "Four Tigers" designation above appears to be a serious oversimplification, making these nations appear to be far more similar than objective scrutiny can justify. To begin with, Hong Kong and Singapore are virtual city-states. Both owe a substantial measure of their success to entrepôt trade, a form of activity that is hardly the basis for the success of Taiwan and South Korea. "Hong Kong and Singapore were founded as trading outposts of the British empire in the nineteenth century" (Sung 1988, 184). Singapore was founded in 1819 and grew rapidly as an entrepôt for trade between Europe and East Asia. The opening of Hong Kong in 1842 cut into Singapore's share of the "China Trade" (184).

"Hong Kong's new political identity must be considered if its current and future economic prospects are to be understood" (McKee, Linn and Chen 1991). Of course Singapore's prospects will be impacted in turn by events involving Hong Kong. By the 1960s and 1970s Hong Kong had adjusted its economic base from a reliance upon entrepôt trade for virtually all of its exports to a situation where "it was arguably the world's most dynamic center of light industry" (McKee et al. 1991, referring to *The Economist*, Survey of Hong Kong, 1989, 7). According to *The Economist*, by the early 1970s Hong Kong had become "a minor industrial power in its own right" (1989, 7). However, at present, "Other jurisdictions are able to produce various goods more cheaply than Hong Kong. . . . Currently the trend is towards a shift in light manufacturing activity . . . to locations within China" (McKee et al. 1991). Of course the output from such ventures may be exported through Hong Kong, and the former colony may once again resume its function as an entrepôt (1991).

Assuming a smooth transition in governance in 1997, Hong Kong's role as a catalyst to trade between the international economy and China should insure its ongoing economic vitality. It has been an international financial center and a provider of services to the international business community. By continuing those functions it may well be instrumental in facilitating and strengthening trans-Pacific linkages as China enlarges its dealings with the developed world.

Singapore too has become a significant supplier of services for international business. "Located at the hub of South-East Asia along strategic waterways and lacking any significant natural resource endowments Singapore has developed as a regional centre, providing many services to neighboring countries" (Tucker and Sundberg 1988, 117). In addition to services, the nation has opted to encourage manufacturing for export. Writing in 1990, Marcus Noland reported progress in electronics and chemical industries and attempts at attracting foreign direct investment in other sophisticated manufacturing activities (26). He saw Singapore as a potential beneficiary from uncertainties facing Hong Kong and alluded to efforts on the part of the government to encourage "Singapore's development as the international financial center of Southeast Asia, as an alternative to Hong Kong" (26). Though such an alternative may not be needed, the fact that a second major international service center is emerging in the region may well facilitate a further expansion in trans-Pacific business and economic linkages.

Singapore comes to an international perspective quite naturally. After its emergence early in the nineteenth century it quickly became a major link between Europe and Asia. Its position at the mouth of the Straits of Malacca gave it strategic importance. It became both a port for merchant ships and a base for naval power. Indeed, "it became Britain's chief base in the Orient" and at the beginning of World War II "was the chief Western Stronghold in Asia" (Elegant 1990, 172).

According to Elegant, "Singapore is virtually unique as a trading nation" (176). By 1987 its exports exceeded its gross domestic product, and its total trade was three times its internal output of goods and services (176). It serves as a port for the Malaysian peninsula as well as a regional processing center. As Elegant suggests, "Singapore's prosperity is based primarily upon two enterprises, electronics and oil, as well as its vast entrepot trade" (192). However, its role as an international service center is expanding, a circumstance that may well expand its trans-Pacific interests.

The remaining Tigers, Taiwan and South Korea, are larger. What they have in common with Hong Kong and Singapore is the fact that they have based their expansion plans upon exports. *The Economist* proclaimed Taiwan and South Korea to be societies addicted to growth (1989, 12). According to Elegant, Taiwan in the early 1950s was an impoverished and demoralized pauper state, incapable even of making its own rifles (1990, 20). Its progress has been based largely upon manufacturing. "Between 1953 and 1987, agriculture's share of GDP fell from 38.3 percent to 6.1 percent, while manufacturing's share rose from 17.7 percent to 47.5 percent, the highest in the world (Noland 1990, 32). Noland cites an extraordinary parallel increase in the share of international trade in national income: to 60.7 percent in 1987 (32). He points out that the United States by itself accounted for more than 25 percent of Taiwan's domestic output in that year. Thus, Taiwan has forged a major trans-Pacific trading link.

Taiwan's chief trading port, Kaohsiung, is the third largest container port in the world (Elegant 1990, 38). It contains "more than two thousand factories operating and more being built to produce plastics and paints, ships and steel, machine tools, fertilizer, chemicals, and petroleum" (38). This figure "did not include additional thousands of small plants that made parts for motorcycles, tractors, pumps, flashlights, radios, and hundreds of other light industrial products" (38). Excluded as well were "hundreds of small plants processing foodstuffs or brewing oyster sauce, shrimp paste, soya sauce, chili oil and other condiments" (38). Thus it seems clear that Taiwan has staked its economic future upon the export of manufactured goods and that trans-Pacific trade is an important component of that strategy.

Elegant sees South Korea's prospects for the future as brilliant and as even better than Taiwan's (1990, 54). Indeed, others have suggested that "Korea can no longer be thought of as an underdeveloped country" (Hamilton and Tanter 1987, 76). Elegant attributes the success of both Taiwan and Korea to markets in the United States (70). He cites the export of automobiles to the United States, an undertaking which was nonexistent in 1985 and had risen to more than 800,000 sales by 1989 (70). "As in Taiwan, sales abroad fueled the extraordinary rise of the Korean Economy—again primarily sales to the United States" (70). He pointed out that 40 percent of Korean exports went to the United States in 1988, a year when exports accounted for one-third of the GNP (70). Clearly, trans-Pacific trade has become an important factor in Korea's economic expansion.

It would appear as though all four Tigers have benefitted from trans-Pacific trade. Hong Kong has become a special case because of its impending change of status. That adjustment may very well raise the level of trans-Pacific trade emanating from Hong Kong if that jurisdiction becomes a window on the world for China's growing economy. Both Hong Kong and Singapore seem destined to improve their positions as international service centers. Unlike these two city-states, Taiwan and Korea have placed their major emphasis upon manufacturing for export. In both cases significant portions of those exports traverse the Pacific to enter markets in the United States. Clearly, all four economies are in debt to the changes in transportation and communications, not to mention the emergent cadres of business services that have facilitated the trans-Pacific access that has permitted them to join the ranks of the newly industrialized countries.

## EMERGING ECONOMIES

In the wake of the Tigers, four other Asian economies have emerged as major participants in the Pacific theater of operations. These are Indonesia, Malaysia, the Philippines and Thailand. Like the Tigers before them, they have had to rely upon foreign linkages to encourage their development. In this regard their emerging success has been fueled by advances in transportation and communications and of course by various services that facilitate business. Their success has focused additional attention upon the Pacific Rim.

In some circles there has been talk of the existence of a fifth Asian Tiger. Thailand, which has been dubbed "the hub of mainland South East Asia" (Schlosstein 1991, 137), is increasingly being considered as sharing in the "economic miracle" that the Tigers have accomplished. The nation's rapid economic growth during the 1960s can be attributed for the most part to United States military expenditures occasioned by the war in Vietnam (141).

Despite the boost that the economy received during the war period, Thailand today is linked more closely to Japan than to the United States in economic and business terms. "In 1985 Japan accounted for 26.7 percent of all foreign investment in Thailand, but by 1988 it was more than half. (America's share slipped from 16.6 percent of the total to less than 10 percent over the same period.)" (145). Thailand's economy is geared to export and has benefitted from Japan's recent strategy of moving lower value-added production to weaker currency countries (152).

According to Schlosstein, the United States, Japan and Singapore account for nearly half of the nation's total exports (154–55). On the import side Japan accounts for nearly a third of the traffic, with the United States a distant second at 14 percent (155). Although Thailand is very much in the Japanese economic orbit, some of its trade does span the Pacific. Like most of the nations discussed in this chapter, it must rely upon external linkages to insure its economic future.

To the south of Thailand sits Asia's least-industrialized economy, Malaysia (Schlosstein 1991, 284). Writing in 1988, Tucker and Sundberg suggested that "Malaysia's rapid growth in the 1970's, fueled by the boom in oil and primary commodity export earnings, has hastened the nation's economic transformation toward a middle income industrializing country" (83). Schlosstein has described the economy of Malaysia as "a tale of many commodities," notably palm oil, rubber and tin "for which it is either the world's number one producer or its largest exporter" (1991, 222). Beyond such outputs he reports that "Kuala Lumpur and . . . Penang have become microelectronic production hubs for both Japanese and American manufacturers" (222). As is the case with Thailand, Japan is Malaysia's major trading partner. The potential for an expanded trans-Pacific trade remains to be seen.

Among the economies under discussion, Indonesia is potentially a force to be reckoned with. As Elegant has suggested, it "impresses with its size and its diversity" (1990, 219). He went on to point to it as the sixth-largest political entity in the world and the fifth-largest producer in OPEC. "Its total exports . . . are three-quarters agricultural and mineral: timber and rubber; tin, bauxite, and nickel; as well as oil" (219). Despite that heavy primary emphasis, "almost a fifth of . . . exports are now manufactured goods, chiefly textiles, steel, and plywood" (219).

According to Schlosstein, "What kicked the Indonesian economy into high gear was the war between Israel and Egypt in October 1972 . . . which catapulted OPEC into power and quadrupled oil prices, practically over-night" (1991, 49). The plight of oil since the mid-1980s has forced the country to encourage a more diversified economy. "In 1988 Indonesia exported $7.7 billion worth of oil and natural gas as against $12.1 billion in nonoil exports" (54). Schlosstein points to average real rates of growth in manufacturing that he considers astounding: "33.8 percent a year be-tween 1982 and 1986; 42.6 percent year-on-year from 1986 to 1987; and 27.1 percent from 1987 to 1988" (54). Such rates were all the more astounding, in his view, because the goods in question were such things as textiles, plywood, iron and steel, footwear, glass and furniture—in other words, goods with significantly high value added (54).

Schlosstein describes Indonesian export markets in 1988 as diverse but predominantly in Asia. "More than two-thirds of Indonesia's exports—69 percent—and over half of its imports, 55 percent, were to and from other nations in East Asia" (56). The United States had major involvements in Indonesia from the 1940s to the 1960s but its role has diminished since then "and sharply in the late 1980's" (Elegant 1990, 236). Thus Indonesia's export orientation can hardly be considered as a major boon to trans-Pacific trade and/or linkages.

## SUMMARY

The discussion to date has revealed three groups of independent nations, all of which must consider the Pacific Ocean and their positions with respect to it in any plans that they may have for growth and development. Few if any of the nations concerned can hope for major sustained economic improvement without substantial international linkages. Those with the strongest economies, the Asian Tigers, have actually structured their expan-sion programs around export-oriented activities. In doing so they have been successful in forging strong economic linkages with wealthier nations.

Emerging Asian nations that seem to be following the example of the Tigers are forging linkages with Japan and other Asian trading partners to generate development paths less dependent upon trans-Pacific linkages yet international in scope. In the case of the small island nations of the South Pacific, there can be no development without international linkages. Those nations have been constrained historically by size and in many cases meager resources, not to mention distance. Whether or not improvements in transportation and communications will result in substantially enhanced prospects for economic improvement remains to be seen.

If international linkages are crucial to the development of nations, it seems clear that activities that facilitate those linkages are important on a world scale. Services related to transportation and communications may be the most obvious of such activities, but they alone can hardly be relied upon to facilitate expansion in specific locations. Ever-lengthening lists of service activities facilitate the functioning and growth of the international economy and its components, both industrial and geographic. In some cases international service centers have emerged to house such activities. Notable among those are the financial and business centers of the developed world, for example, London, New York and Tokyo. However, other service centers are emerging. Hong Kong and Singapore are fulfilling various international service functions. Whether other such centers may emerge in the Pacific remains to be seen. Certainly those that exist are strengthening international linkages and thus enhancing development prospects.

# 3

## ACCOUNTING SERVICES AND ECONOMIC EXPANSION

Economic expansion in a nation depends to some degree upon the adequacy of the nation's accounting services. It is possible to envision an economy that has inadequate or unsuitable accounting services that cause a drag on expansion. It is also possible to envision an economy with satisfactory accounting services in which expansion is accelerated because of having these facilitating services available. Accounting services do appear to be a necessary but, of course, not sufficient condition for economic expansion.

Development of accounting services both internal to organizations and in the public arena seems to be evolutionary in nature as economies expand. Historically, although affected by other nations, accounting systems have in the main tended to be country specific. Accounting methods, procedures, and standards have reflected the cultural, legal, political and economic environments and the ways of doing business in each country or region.

Accounting services demanded appear in general to increase in breadth and depth as economic expansion occurs. Services found in a poorer economy are of course quite different from those necessary for an advanced economy.[1] As economies expand, standards for reporting accounting and financial information to governments and to the public seem to become increasingly codified. Accounting-related accoutrements and infrastructures expand. The numbers of accounting practitioners and their educational levels tend to increase.

In the public accounting sector, partnerships are formed and expanded. Accounting professional associations are organized and increasingly developed at the local, national and international levels. The professional body of knowledge expands.

Accounting education takes on ever-increasing sophistication and complexity. Government regulation, either direct or through professional groups, becomes more exacting. Licensing of public accountants seems to become necessary and more difficult to attain and maintain.

Accounting services internal to organizations seem to follow a similar evolutionary process in breadth and depth. Instead of public accounting partnership expansion, companies institute and expand the internal audit functions as well as increase the cadres of accountants employed.

Accounting reports become more complex. Managers, investors, and other users of accounting information need to become better able to understand and to profit from accounting products. As economic development progresses, successful business operations must increasingly, it seems, be carried on across national borders. Business managers and investors alike are at pains to be knowledgeable and competent users of information products of ever more integrated and growing global marketplaces.

Information needed may in many instances be prepared on a global basis. Information created and used within a multinational corporation may be an example, identically created wherever the company operates, making information analysis and decision making within the organization and across national borders more effective and efficient. Yet as operations are carried on in foreign countries, their laws, cultures and ways of doing business, which may radically differ, must be considered. Understanding these differing characteristics and related information products is almost certainly necessary for success.

Internal systems to produce accounting and financial reports may be global, particularly if controlled by such organizations as multinational corporations. However, in many reporting systems, information in all likelihood takes on regional or country-specific characteristics. Although multinational corporations can control their own internal accounting and reporting, external reporting is generally influenced if not controlled by governments or their designees or by other users of such information.

In addition, accounting and reporting standards may require differing kinds of treatments, depending upon the differing natures of the economic and business environments in countries in which the corporation operates. This suggests that two aspects of accounting reporting be considered as economies expand: Who controls the authority to set accounting and reporting standards, and what effects do varying economic conditions and differing business arrangements have on the way accounting and reporting is done? The latter conditions may superimpose information needs that the former have no choice but to follow.

Prior to the 1970s, accounting standards were the exclusive province of individual nations, in which government regulators either set standards directly or delegated the task to national accounting professional associations, generally with oversight by government. Competitive international pressures caused by the great expansion of capital markets created an international "need for financial information that could be understood and compared by competitors (Collins 1989, 82)" in whatever nation prepared or used it.

Because standard-setting authority is nation-specific, the needs for cross-border information could not and cannot be met by a single nation. In 1973 a group of national standard setters formed the International Accounting Standards Committee (IASC), with the purpose of improving harmonization of national accounting standards. By 1992 the IASC had grown to include professional bodies from seventy-eight countries as members (*CPA Journal* 1992, 16).

Although some progress has been made through IASC efforts, there is still no single global system by which public accounting and financial reporting is accomplished in all parts of the world. In fact, accounting systems remain largely nation-state specific. Each nation or confederation of states, such as the European Economic Community (EEC), retains legal right and authority to establish and operate standards of accounting and financial reporting for all within its jurisdiction.[2] A multinational corporation may dictate accounting and reporting requirements within its structures, but within a nation-state's jurisdiction the corporation must comply with requirements set by that state.

Being country specific and arising from the culture, laws, customs and ways of doing business in each country or region, accounting and reporting systems naturally differ radically across the globe. A knowledgeable user of financial information in a given country discovers that information prepared under foreign principles is radically divergent from that which is customary in his home country. Likewise, the accountant in one nation finds that audit requirements may differ, ways and means of setting audit and accounting standards differ, legal requirements differ among nations.[3]

Both preparers and users of accounting information have a substantial job in mastering country-specific conditions and requirements under which the information has been created. Yet such understanding must be attained if analysis and decision making are to be successful.

Although public investors and creditors are generally the focus of discussions on the uses of improved accounting and reporting systems, Shaun F. O'Malley (1992, 28), president of the Financial Accounting Foundation, in viewing the need for comparable statements from a corporate perspective discussed some important areas of business and finance in which comparable financial statements aid a business in evaluating its own strengths and weaknesses.

Businesses need to conduct "competitive surveillance" (28) of growing foreign businesses by using foreign financial statements in comparison with their own. Relationships of the business to customers, suppliers and potential foreign business partners is vital to maintain maximum flexibility of operations. The financial wherewithal of foreign customers or the potential of alternative suppliers needs to be assessed. In the processes of raising capital abroad or in investing in foreign securities, corporate officials need understanding of foreign financial statements in managing investments or in raising capital. Finally, O'Malley observes that without comparable statements it would be extremely difficult to have a clear understanding of the "relative profitability, liquidity, and financial staying power" (28) of one's own business in relation to foreign competition.

The arrangements by which capital is allocated seem to have substantial influence on accounting and reporting requirements. In countries where capital allocation decisions are made primarily in large capital markets, the objective of accounting and reporting systems is to provide information for decisions by a large pool of creditors and investors. The emphasis in these countries is to disclose adequate information to allow informed decisions by market participants, thereby allocating capital to best uses.

Full and fair disclosure is the goal of the accounting and reporting system. As capital is allocated by creditors and investors in open markets, companies operating in this environment naturally are concerned with demonstrating investment quality and earning power and potential. In these capital market based countries, the accounting and public reporting system is of great interest to a wide variety of concerned stakeholders.

In other countries capital may be controlled by a small number of banks that can arrange to receive information needed directly from the businesses to which capital is allocated. The importance of public disclosure is greatly diminished. There appears to be little need for full and fair public disclosure in these countries. The public accounting and reporting requirements seem to be designed more to demonstrate compliance with government regulations and tax laws. As capital is not allocated through an open market system, there is little need to demonstrate earnings power to a large number of market participants. Consequently accounting standards tend to be conservative.

In still other countries where inflation has been persistent and at high levels, standard-setting authorities have adopted procedures and reporting requirements to reflect the impacts of changing purchasing-power monetary measures. In these countries accounting systems are more geared to the needs of taxing authorities and to governmental planners.[4]

Perhaps a global system for public reporting is beyond even distance reach. Business conditions and customs in different parts of the world may prohibit global standardization. Some would say that a global standard is not needed or appropriate because of differences among countries. Most agree that harmonization at least is needed, and some think it critically needed.

As indicated above, the International Accounting Standards Committee includes representatives from the various national professional bodies and was formed to assist in improving international financial reporting and in harmonizing national standards. From its inception to about 1987, the IASC seemed to be intent on eliminating bad reporting practices by reducing the number of acceptable alternative accounting treatments in the divergent accounting systems of the world. As Arthur Wyatt (*CPA Journal* 1992, 18) explained, "A vote of 11 out of 14 members is needed to pass an IASC standard. In order to get that many to agree, in its initial stages, IASC often had to accept the two most popular practices in a particular area in order to get 11 votes" (16). The most popular practices thereby survived. But even with this narrowing of choices, too many alternative treatments for important, material transactions still caused International Accounting Standards-based financial statements to lack comparability.

Just one example should illustrate the problem. International Accounting Standard Number 22 (International Accounting Standards Committee 1991, AC 9022.40) allows expensing of goodwill over the useful life of the goodwill, which is similar to the U.S. provisions, or goodwill may be immediately written off against stockholders' equity in a fashion similar to the U.K. provisions. Obviously, substantially different earnings numbers are reported, depending upon the option selected.

A report in the *Journal of Accountancy* (1989, 85) indicated that "financial statements of most entities conformed in all material respects with IASC standards and that, in most nations, national practices conformed with 23 of 25 existing IASC standards" (85). This meant little, as the alternatives contained in the International Accounting Standards literally allowed most country standards to be in conformity even though resulting financial statements could not be relied upon to be usefully comparable.

A statement by Ralph E. Walters, chairman of the steering committee of the IASC, highlights the problem: "Our global markets cannot continue much longer to put up with provincial financial reporting. Burgeoning international markets put both internal and external pressures on national standard setters to adopt a global view" (Collins 1989, 82).

Shaun F. O'Malley, chairman and senior partner of Price Waterhouse and president of the Financial Accounting Foundation, also believes the problem to be serious. "International comparability of financial statements is the most important accounting issue facing businesses today" (O'Malley 1992, 28). And, he suggests one path to improvement for international accounting: "Setting broad standards that preserve country-specific rules and harmonize country-to-country differences would go a long way toward meeting this challenge" (28).

There seems little doubt that those who operate the world's capital markets have a pressing need for financial reports that will be comparable across national borders. Capital markets are of course governed by national authorities. In some nations disclosure and accounting requirements necessary to be listed on exchanges are more stringent than in other countries. This causes exchanges with less stringent and presumably less costly requirements to have a comparative advantage in attracting business.

The New York Stock Exchange, for example, which must abide by U.S. requirements, the most stringent and costly in the world, is at a disadvantage to other exchanges that accept less costly and stringent standards, for example, International Accounting Standards–based reports. Foreign companies seeking to raise capital in the U.S. must issue financial disclosures consistent with U.S. generally accepted accounting principles (GAAP) or reconcile their foreign results to GAAP standards in footnotes. Arthur Wyatt reported that "No other country in the world has such a requirement for foreign companies wishing to raise capital in their borders" (1992, 52).

James A. Heely and Roy L Nersesian (1993), in discussing the desire on the part of capital markets for comparable accounting reports, observed that "One driving force to develop a global accounting system is the desire to underwrite securities in any, or all, of the world's capital markets using a single set of financial statements" (1993, 81). This incentive and the fact that "globalization of corporate activity, coupled with economic and political integration of large groupings of nations, are engines of change in accounting practices" (81) led Heely and Nersesian to comment that "opponents to a global accounting system certainly can delay the process, but they may not be able to prevent its eventual success" (81).

The capital markets' underwriting incentives are reflected in International Organization of Securities Commissions (IOSCO) positions. The IOSCO indicated in the late 1980s that International Accounting Standards' optional accounting treatments need to be reduced to produce an accounting product that can be used in international trading of securities. Further, if an acceptable, quality system of accounting is developed it appears that the IOSCO will encourage its member-country securities regulators to require all nondomestic issuers to present financial statements in accordance with International Accounting Standards (*CPA Journal* 1992, 18).

Partly in response to this pressure, the IASC began to reduce the options in International Accounting Standards, to establish benchmarks where choices are allowed, and to improve disclosure through a comparability and improvement project begun in 1988. The committee "identified 25 alternatives which it felt should and could be eliminated" (18). According to Arthur Wyatt, the project would cover "80 percent of the alternatives in its existing standards" (1992, 51). The project was completed in 1993 with the revision of ten International Accounting Standards (*Journal of Accountancy*, 1994, 23).

As a result IOSCO is in the process of considering the endorsement of the revised statements. To further the development of an acceptable international accounting system, IOSCO has agreed upon a list of "necessary components of a reasonably complete set of core standards for cross-border offerings and listings" (1994, 24).

The results of these efforts remain to be seen. But if they are successful, the current situation in which a plethora of country-specific standards must now be used in international trade will give way to perhaps only two kinds of standards. As Arthur Wyatt observes, "a securities regulator in a particular country would need to know only two systems of accounting—its own and international standards" (*CPA Journal* 1992, 18). The same could be said for the companies who prepare and the many stakeholders who use financial statements for international commerce.

The revised International Accounting Standards, it appears, will not only be a system in which accounting options have been reduced but will be a system designed for international capital markets. It may be a system that IOSCO and their individual country securities regulators will view as a quality accounting system that can be used in the trading of international securities. Such a result is a needed and beneficial one. Yet the transformation of International Accounting Standards may make them less useful for domestic adoption in individual nations.

Some developing countries have adopted the International Accounting Standards either completely or with some adaptations as their national accounting standards. By joining IASC and adopting its pronouncements, the country reduces the costs to develop and maintain the accounting structure. The adoption of International Accounting Standards demonstrates that the country encourages growth of foreign investments, has joined the movement toward harmonization of accounting standards and is a "full-fledged member of the international community" (Riahi-Belkaoui 1994, 37).

The downside of such national adoption has been that International Accounting Standards do not meet the domestic needs of the developing country as well as might more situation-specific accounting rules. As Riahi-Belkaoui observed, "the international standards for accounting for various transactions occurring in the advanced countries may be totally irrelevant to some of the developing countries" (1994, 37). He suggests that many types of transactions in the developed world have little chance of occurring in the developing countries and that transaction types similar to those in a developed country that do occur are in the "context of the developing country" (37). Further, "the institutional and market factors of these countries are different enough in some contexts to justify a more 'situationist' approach to standard setting" (37).

One of the primary problems in the past for International Accounting Standards has been that the many alternatives allowed resulted in standards that had little meaning in conveying business and financial information in ways that allowed users to have confidence that comparisons between entities were reliable. Certainly the concerns of Shaun F. O'Malley and Ralph E. Walters, discussed above, for comparable information across national borders must be applicable for reporting within a nation. It would also seem that the uses, described above by O'Malley, to which businesses put accounting information for cross-border commerce would be equally needed within a nation.

It seems doubtful that International Accounting Standards as compiled in the past were able to meet the needs for a quality accounting system in developing countries. It is questionable whether future International Accounting Standards designed for international use will meet the domestic needs of a given developing country. Several of the many reasons why this may be so are discussed below.

Capital may be allocated by government or a small number of banks. A well-developed capital market may not exist. Under these conditions, full-disclosure principles used in advanced countries to inform the large number of investors and creditors may not be needed or appropriate. The providers of capital, be they government or private, can usually require the information they need in the form needed. For these and perhaps other reasons, widespread full-disclosure principles may not be desired in a given country.

In many developing countries the governmental sector looms large. Government goals may call for domestic accounting and reporting systems suitable for country-specific use which may differ from international needs. More central planning and other types of government interventions in the economy often result in governmental requirements being imposed on the accounting system. The tax collection and law enforcement systems internal to developing countries may be expected to require accounting systems that differ from systems using international standards. In some cases, governments for internal reasons may dictate private-sector financial reporting systems that are consistent with tax or other legal systems regardless of economic measurement accuracy. In other countries, the private-sector firms may choose to use the same accounting systems for tax and financial reporting purposes. The benefits of maintaining two accounting systems may not be viewed as worth the cost.

Some countries have a relatively low level of economic activity in general. Some may have low levels of commerce with foreign countries. Their domestic need for accounting information and disclosure may be correspondingly lower than that under international accounting standards. In countries where the population is small, there are fewer people to be interested in development of the accounting system or able to devote time and resources to such development.

Within a country, then, whatever the stage of economic expansion, even though the improved International Accounting Standards may assist those making decisions about international commerce, it is not clear that a satisfactory domestic accounting system and related accounting services can be built solely on international standards for use when making domestic decisions. Judging by past arrangements within countries, it would appear that, whatever the state of international reporting, individual countries can be expected to need a more situation-specific set of domestic accounting standards.

But it must be remembered that accounting systems based on domestic needs internal to countries, particularly developing countries, do not appear to be an acceptable solution for attracting international flows of capital. Peavey and Webster put the problem with clarity: "For developing countries to be competitive in world capital markets, they need more widely accepted accounting standards" (1990, 32). Further, they believe, "Local companies in less developed countries cannot expect to be knowledgeable about the accounting requirements in each of the capital markets that otherwise might be available to them" (32). Thus, it may be that economic expansion, global and country specific, may be better facilitated by accounting services with two sets of characteristics—international and domestic.

Of course, it remains to be seen whether revised International Accounting Standards will be taken up as a global standard by the various countries in which the decision rests. But, once an accounting system that meets the needs of international users does emerge, some believe that countries will have great incentive to adopt the system for international use lest their companies be at a disadvantage in attracting capital and lest their capital markets be at a disadvantage in attracting underwriting business.

A further fundamental aspect should be considered. If investors and creditors do not have confidence in the accuracy, truthfulness and fairness of accounting reports, they will not invest absent insider information. John M. Livingstone believes that "A flourishing stock exchange implies a high standard of accuracy and honesty in reporting" (1990, 33). He argues that for some countries, particularly Third World countries, changes needed are not just that of a better international reporting system but of a cultural change in values. Tax evasion and the keeping of two or three sets of books for differing purposes is the norm in some countries. He believes that "It is not too easy to create a stock exchange as a means of funneling savings into industry in a society where tax evasion, bribery and any other practice which cannot be presented openly in accounts is the norm" (33). The potential investor is unlikely to provide capital under such circumstances. Further, available global capital can be expected to tend to flow toward countries where these conditions do not exist, thereby determining the contours and areas for economic expansion.

To the extent that quality audit practices are in place, the potential investor can be expected to have more confidence in accounting reports and disclosures. Audit practices and standards in the various countries differ but do not exhibit the wide dispersion found in accounting standards. Indicative of the comparability of auditing standards was an analysis by McKee and Garner (1992, 31–33) in which thirty-three of forty-five countries were thought to have auditing standards comparable to standards in the U.S. in 1986.

The International Federation of Accountants' International Auditing Practices Committee (IAPC) since 1977 has been responsible for promulgating standards to improve comparability among national requirements for audit and reporting. The IAPC has issued twenty-nine International Standards on Auditing. Guidelines have also been issued on review, agreed-upon procedures and compilation engagements.[5]

In its publication of *International Accounting and Auditing Standards* the American Institute of Certified Public Accountants (1991) included at the end of each International Standard on Auditing a comparison with U.S. generally accepted auditing standards. These comparisons in general indicate that the international standards are more demanding in some respects and cover some topics that U.S. audit standards do not. Thus, it seems reasonable to think that International Standards on Auditing provide a basis for quality audit in the world, both developed and developing.

The environments and conditions of the auditing, accounting and reporting systems in the various Pacific Rim countries can be expected to follow the evolutionary processes described above. One would expect that accounting and reporting standards have been established by the individual nation-states. One would expect that they are designed to meet country-specific conditions and to be consistent with the laws, cultures and ways of doing business within each country.

It would seem that the depth and breadth of the accounting and reporting systems can be expected to vary to some extent with the degree of economic expansion experienced by each country. In some developing countries that have large populations, such as India, Pakistan and Egypt, there are higher numbers of people who are interested in better accounting systems (Riahi-Belkaoui 1994, 32). Thus, a given Pacific Rim nation may have more highly developed accounting services than one would expect at its stage of economic expansion.

## NOTES

1. See Ahmed Riahi-Belkaoui (1994) for an extended discussion of accounting in developing countries.

2. See Larry L. Orsini and Lawrence R. Hudack (1992, 20) for a discussion of EEC accounting issues.

3. See McKee and Garner (1992) for a more extensive analysis.

4. See also Gerhard G. Mueller, Helen Gernon, and Gary Meek (1991) for analysis of accounting principles developmental models.

5. See also Heely and Nersesian (1993, 82–89).

# PART II

## INSTITUTIONAL PARAMETERS FOR ACCOUNTING PRACTICE

# 4

## ACCOUNTING ENVIRONMENTS IN SELECTED NEWLY INDUSTRIALIZED ASIAN ECONOMIES

Among the economies in question, variations in accounting practices based upon how they became linked to the international economy might be expected. In Hong Kong and Singapore one would expect accounting and business practice to be influenced by institutions and procedures inherited from the British. In South Korea and Taiwan, United States influence might be perceived to be more prevalent.

### REPUBLIC OF KOREA

In the Republic of Korea all businesses except for the very small are required by the Commercial Code to maintain proper accounting books, a shareholder register and minutes books. Company managements are held accountable for such records and reports. Generally accepted accounting principles (GAAP) are formulated by the Ministry of Finance (MOF) and by the Korean Securities and Exchange Commission (SEC). They take the form of decrees and MOF regulations and are binding upon all businesses, including single proprietorships. If financial accounting standards do not contain applicable prescriptions, accountants and auditors may fall back on other laws and regulations or on procedures established through general practice. For instance, Korean GAAP is affected in many areas by principles of taxation (Coopers and Lybrand 1991, K-1).

Organizations that engage in profit-seeking commercial transactions may take the sole proprietor form. Under the Korean Commercial Code, forms of commercial organization may be incorporated. These include two forms of partnership—a general commercial partnership with unlimited liability for members and a "limited partnership" where some members have unlimited liability while for others liability is limited. Beyond partnership arrangements, a private company can be formed with total membership normally limited to fifty persons. In such arrangements, members' liability is limited to what they have contributed for units in the firm. Although units can be transferred, such transactions require general membership approval.

Joint stock companies are also permitted. For such forms shareholders' liability is limited to the amount contributed for the purchase of shares. Shares can be transferred by rule. Most Korean companies follow this joint stock format. All incorporated businesses in Korea must publish year-end balance sheets in a public newspaper (KPMG San Tong and Co. 1990, 27–29).

The Korean Commercial Code requires every incorporated entity to appoint a statutory auditor. Corporations with total assets in excess of W3 billions or with paid-in capital in excess of W500 million require an audit by an independent licensed Korean CPA (5). Independent auditor's examinations are intended to provide the basis for an opinion on whether the financial statements give a true and fair view of the firm's financial standing and on whether the results of operations are in compliance with the Korean GAAP. The External Audit Law regulates the size and number of companies that a CPA may audit.

Various corporations have been exempted, including those subject to the Law on Management of Government-related Corporations. Also exempted are those who have gotten half of their equity in capital from local municipalities and those structured as an exemption to the outside audit by the MOF in consultation with the SEC.

Beyond audits for financial reporting purposes, the tax returns of certain companies should be reviewed and certified before they are filed (Price Waterhouse 1992b, 93). The External Audit Supervisory Commission, a department of the SEC, has the responsibility to ensure compliance with auditing standards. Audit procedures follow English-speaking-country standards and are intended to insure uniformity and objectivity and independence. The Korean auditor's report is similar to the U.S. standard short-form report issued prior to the 1988 revision (88). To undertake audit engagements, membership in the Korean Institute of Certified Public Accountants is required. Established in 1954, the institute boasted a membership of 2,188 registered CPAs, six foreign CPAs and 351 junior CPAs as of the end of 1989 (KPMG, San Tong and Co. 1990, 3–4).

Applicants for membership must pass the Korean CPA examination, which is controlled by the SEC. According to Price Waterhouse the examinations are difficult, with roughly 250 passing each year (1992b, 88). In 1992 there were upwards of 2,000 CPAs in practice. Although much in demand, CPAs were in short supply. The requirements for registration of CPA firms are strict (88). Foreign CPAs are restricted to auditing joint ventures in which an entity from the CPA's home country invests 50 percent or more. However, they may also audit companies in which the CPA's firm has an interest or association with a South Korean CPA (KPMG Tong and Co. 1990, 2) or as requested by the South Korean government.

The Korean Institute of Certified Public Accountants has put forward rules of ethics and professional conduct. Among such regulations are restrictions of conduct with respect to commissions, advertising, beneficial interest of clients and unfair competition. Ongoing professional education is also required of members.

Korean accounting principles are promulgated by the SEC, subject to the approval of the Ministry of Finance. The SEC is assisted by the Accounting Standards Advisory Board of the Institute and by the Bank of Korea. All companies in the nation are required to comply with the accounting standards. Financial reports prepared under Korean GAAP require more detailed information than do those prepared under U.S. or U.K. GAAP.

There are various other differences between Korean and United States standards. Revaluation of assets is permitted under specific circumstances. Asset valuation is originally recorded at acquisition costs but may be revalued. Allocation of revenues and costs to specific accounting periods differs in various ways from U.S. GAAP. Marketable securities and security investments are valued at the lower of cost or market using a weighted-average or moving-average method. The investments of affiliated companies over which the parent has significant influences can be carried at cost even if the market is below cost value.

Goodwill is capitalized and amortized over an estimated useful life of between five and ten years (Bavishi 1991, 53). Negative goodwill is entered as an addition to paid-in capital. Certain costs can be deferred and amortized over three to five years: organizational, preoperating, new stock issuance, debenture issuance and certain defined research and development costs.

A legal reserve of 10 percent must be set aside until 50 percent of total capital stock is reached. Conglomerates in Korea are more in the nature of brother-sister relationships than parent-subsidiary relationships (Price Waterhouse 1992b, 93). Korean consolidated financial statements often fail to provide adequate disclosures with respect to such relationships. According to Bavishi, consolidated statements include only majority-owned domestic subsidiaries, with others reported generally at cost (1991, 54). He also pointed out that equity-method procedures are not required for investments in affiliates over which the parent has substantial control, except in cases where consolidated financial statements are prepared (53).

In Korea accounting changes are handled prospectively, never retroactively. Depreciation and bad debt expenses may be calculated by tax rules that may not reflect the basis that most closely reflects economic activity. Although segment reporting by industry is not required, reporting by product lines is followed by many firms. Allocation of income tax between periods is not permitted. Differences in classification criteria dictate that most leases be carried as operating leases. Depreciation of leased assets is booked over lease term length rather than economic useful life (Price Waterhouse 1992b, 95). Foreign currency translations use the current rate method, with gains or losses taken to the income statement or to shareholders' equity (Bavishi 1991, 53). Interim reports are semiannual in nature and are not on a consolidated basis. Clearly a wide range of differences exists between Korean and United States accounting and reporting standards.

## TAIWAN

In Taiwan business enterprises can be organized as single proprietorships, partnerships, or companies. Only Chinese are permitted to operate single proprietorships, while aliens can engage in partnerships or hold company shares. In terms of liability of shareholders four corporate categories exist: unlimited, limited, unlimited with limited liability stockholders, and limited by share (Soong 1992, 19). Unlimited company shareholders are liable for all company obligations. Limited companies, with from five to twenty-one shareholders, have liabilities limited to capital contributions. Unlimited companies with limited-liability shareholders must have one or more shareholders with unlimited liability. For companies limited by shares, the liability of shareholders is limited to the amount of subscribed capital shares.

Legal reserves equal to 10 percent of annual net profits must be withheld until they equal the amount of capital stock authorized. The building of such a reserve takes precedence over dividends and/or bonus payments. Company shares are not normally redeemable by the company.

Foreign companies may apply to the Ministry of Economic Affairs to conduct business in Taiwan by establishing a branch, by having a local agent or by establishing a liaison officer. Qualified foreign investors, including foreign companies, may establish a domestic company or a foreign-investment-approved company. Investors in foreign-investment approved companies are permitted free repatriation of invested capital and net profits, the waiver of domicile and nationality requirements and other considerations (24).

Companies with paid-in capital of NT $200 million or more can be registered by the Securities and Exchange Commission (SEC) of Taiwan as public companies. Such firms need not be listed on a stock exchange but must make a public disclosure of their financial statements. Companies with paid-in capital exceeding NT $200 million are generally required to offer shares to the public. A company going public must have audited financial statements for three years and a reconciliation of financial statement income with taxable income certified by a CPA. The CPA's comments on company internal control are also required (23). The financial statements for companies traded publicly must follow SEC regulations, which are generally the same as GAAP in Taiwan (25).

As early as 1981 joint multiprofession committees involving CPA associations were established to help in meeting the demand for professional accounting expertise and services. The Financial Accounting Committee was charged with establishing and updating general accounting principles. In 1985 the CPAs of Taiwan established the Accounting Research and Development Foundation. That organization took responsibility for the Financial Accounting Committee, renaming it the Financial Accounting Standards Committee. Beyond accounting practitioners the committee also includes representation from the governmental, business and academic spheres. The committee formulates generally accepted accounting principles, which then enjoy strong government support and are widely followed.

A Code of Professional Ethics for CPAs and a series of related ethics standards applying to CPAs in public practice has been issued through the National Federation of CPA Associations. In addition to adherence to acceptable ethical standards, continuing professional education is required for CPAs.

As of January 1991 there were approximately 2,100 CPAs in Taiwan, of whom 43 percent were registered as public accounting practitioners. Of the practitioners, 508 were working on their own while 401 were associated with some 75 CPA partnerships (5).

Company managements are responsible for keeping proper financial records and for the proper preparation of financial reports to insure fair presentations to both shareholders and tax authorities. With the exception of computerized systems and small-scale enterprises, accounting books must be submitted to the tax authority for registration before use. Computerized systems must be approved by the tax authority.

All entries for transactions require the support of proper documents. For the purchase of goods or services a unified invoice prescribed and controlled by the tax authority represents the primary documentation. The tax authority holds strict control over invoice forms through printing, prenumbering and binding.

Companies with capital of NT $30 million are required to have audited financial statements. Those with bank credit reaching NT $30 million must submit the audit report and financial statements to the Credit Center of the Taipei Bankers' Association. Those with revenues of NT $100 million must have their income tax returns certified by a CPA. Other companies may have their income tax returns certified on a voluntary basis, thus cutting the risk of tax authority investigations (10).

Publicly held companies must submit audited annual financial statements and audited semiannual financial statements, as well as first and third quarter financial statements (reviewed by CPAs) to the SEC. These materials must also be published in newspapers. For listed and over-the-counter companies these reports must also be provided to the Stock Exchange and to the Securities Dealers' Association, as well as to the Institute of Securities Market Development (9).

Company managers frequently select the auditor, but their choice may require the approval of the shareholders or the board of directors. Audits of financial statements are subject to the *Regulations Governing the Examination and Certification of Financial Statements by CPAs*, issued jointly by the Ministry of Economic Affairs and the Ministry of Finance. Income tax returns are also audited by CPAs. Such audits are based upon tax regulations (12). Auditing standards in practice are similar to those in the United States. A number of codified auditing standards differences have resulted from changes made in U.S. standards since 1988. The Taiwan standard audit report is identical to the pre-1988 standard U.S. report.

Taiwan GAAP have been significantly influenced by U.S. accounting pronouncements, but there are some differences of note. Revaluation of assets is permitted, including fixed assets, land, natural resources and intangibles, if prices rise by 25 percent. Depreciation is generally taken on the straight-line basis. Inventory costing generally employs the average-cost method (Bavishi 1991, 88).

Consolidated financial statements are required if one company has control over another, with some exceptions for subsidiaries in businesses so dissimilar as to render consolidations misleading. Legal reorganizations, bankruptcies, and cases of foreign subsidiaries domiciled where dividends cannot be remitted constitute exceptions as well (Soong 1992, 54). A subsidiary with assets or total revenue of less than 10 percent of the parent company may be excluded, as may be a subsidiary with shareholder equity of less than zero.

Business combinations are accounted for under Company Law. Assets and liabilities of the acquired company are generally recorded at their book value. Negative goodwill is charged directly to shareholders' equity (54). The method of accounting for a business combination is not disclosed (Bavishi 1991, 88).

Deferred income tax procedures are not required. Tax-loss carrybacks are not permitted, although carry forwards are allowed under certain conditions. The percentage-of-completion method is required for all long-term construction contracts over one year in which profit or loss can be reasonably estimated. Foreign currency translations are determined by the current rate method, with gains or losses from translation taken into income or deferred (Bavishi 1991, 88). Capital surplus includes such things as premium on capital stock, appraised surplus, gain on disposal of assets, donated capital, and shareholders' equity arising from goodwill from mergers.

Generally accepted accounting principles in Taiwan do not cover several other areas that are addressed in the U.S. Exclusions include earnings per share, disclosure of business segments, futures contracts, development stage enterprises and financial reporting for changing prices (Soong 1992, 18). Some of these items are reported by companies. Bavishi reports that the potential or actual dilution effects on earnings per share of senior convertible securities are not disclosed (1991, 88).

Legal reserves of 10 percent of net after-tax income each year are required to be set aside until the legal reserve reaches 50 percent of paid-in capital. Such reserves can be used only for corporate losses (Price Waterhouse 1991a, 100). Footnotes to financial statements are only sometimes used (Bavishi 1991, 88). As such notes are a principal means of disclosure, this lack may indicate an important difference between Taiwan and more developed country standards of disclosure.

## SINGAPORE

In Singapore business enterprises may take the legal form of an incorporated company—usually with limited liability—may be a branch of a foreign corporation or may be an unincorporated business. The last category may include sole proprietorships, partnerships or joint ventures. The Ministry of Finance through the Registrar of Companies administers companies and securities laws. The Registrar holds required company information and files for public access (David Tong 1993, 25).

Incorporated companies must have records sufficient to explain and support transactions such that financial statements can be prepared reflecting "true and fair" financial condition. Accounting and other records must be available in Singapore for the preparation of true and fair financial statements and for their audit. Public companies must have an adequate system of internal control (97). In Singapore the financial statements of incorporated businesses must be audited by an approved certified public accountant. Branches of foreign corporations must also be audited by approved auditors, who may include qualified auditors from the foreign firm's country of incorporation. There is no statutory audit requirement for unincorporated businesses.

In order to issue either shares or bonds to the public, companies must file a prospectus with the Registrar of Companies (84). Companies can be either private or public. Private companies are limited to fifty shareholders and may restrict the transfer of their shares. A private company with no more than twenty shareholders may be an exempt private company (73). All companies and foreign branches must file annual audited financial statements with the Registrar of Companies. An exception occurs in the case of exempt private companies, which do need audited financial statements but are not required to file those statements with the Registrar (97). Exempt companies may provide the Registrar with a solvency certificate signed by the company secretary and the independent auditor (Coopers and Lybrand 1991, S-2).

The Stock Exchange of Singapore separated from the stock exchange in Malaysia in 1990. It is regulated by the monetary authority under the Securities Industry Act. A second market, the Stock Exchange of Singapore Dealing and Automated Quotation Market, has operated since 1986. It caters to small and medium-size companies with growth potential. Both exchanges have similar reporting and disclosure requirements with required semiannual reports, a preliminary report within three months, and annual audited statements within six months after year close. Listed companies are required to provide information to the exchange for public release, designed to prevent a false market in company shares (61).

The Singapore Accountants Act of 1987 is the primary legislation for the profession. Accountants are viewed as either practicing public accountants or nonpracticing. The nonpracticing category includes those in government and industry and those employed by public accountants.

In 1991 there were 637 public accountants practicing, which represents about 9 percent of the total profession (98). The Accountants Act established the Institute of Public Accountants of Singapore, which is designated as the agency to develop and promulgate accounting and auditing requirements. The act made the Public Accountants Board responsible for registration and disciplining accountants (David Tong 1993). Auditors should be CPAs and members of the institute.

A registered public accountant must have satisfied the requirements set forth in the Public Accountants Board Rules approved by the Minister of Finance and administered by the Institute. Requirements include the completion of the professional examination, requisite experience, preregistration courses and demonstrated proficiency in local laws (2,7).

Auditors are required by the Accountants Act and by the Institute's rules to be independent of audit clients. Public accountants may practice as sole proprietors or in partnerships. Services offered cover a wide range of auditing, accounting, tax, liquidation of companies, corporate secretarial services, and business advisory services (Price Waterhouse 1993c, 98).

Members are obligated to follow the Institute's accounting and auditing standards as well as other pronouncements. The auditing standards set forth by the Institute are essentially international standards adapted as necessary to local circumstances. Generally accepted auditing standards in Singapore are similar to those of the United States. They embrace general standards, standards of field work and reporting standards.

The Companies Act makes necessary a report to the company audit committee on the auditor's review of internal control structure. The auditor's report follows British practice in indicating whether or not the financial statements give a true and fair view of matters reported upon in the financial statements.

Auditors in Singapore report on compliance with requirements of the Companies Act. Any deficiencies that in the auditor's opinion have not been adequately addressed by the client company must be reported to the Registrar of Companies. The auditor is also required to report to the Minister of Finance if serious fraud or dishonesty has been committed against the company. The auditor must provide to trustees of the company's debenture holders the reports issued to the corporation and must also inform those trustees of any matters relevant to the exercise of their duties as trustees (David Tong 1993, 9). According to the Companies Act the company auditor has the right of access at all times to company records. The act provides a penalty for obstructing the completion of an audit (9).

The Institute issues Statements of Accounting Standards, which become mandatory. Singapore has adopted all of the International Accounting Standards Committee's *International Accounting Standards* as the nation's generally accepted accounting procedures. The Institute also issues *Statements of Recommended Accounting Practice*, which accountants may use for guidance. In cases where procedures or practices are not prescribed, generally accepted accounting principles from other countries may be followed.

A number of provisions of the nation's generally accepted accounting principles differ from those of the United States (70). For example, real property can be carried at cost or appraisal value. Appraisal increases are credited to capital reserves. Interest costs incurred while preparing assets for use are not capitalized as part of the cost of the asset.

If control is intended to be temporary, some entities are not consolidated even if control is assured. Controlled entities for which long-term restrictions on the transfers of funds exist are not consolidated. Unconsolidated subsidiaries are carried at cost, revaluation amounts, or the lower of cost or market. Goodwill may be recognized as an asset, amortized over its useful life or written off against shareholders' interest (72).

Imputed interest methods are not used for receivables or payables that are not subject to normal trade terms (75). Separate reporting for discontinued segments of a business is not required (80). Operating losses for Singapore income tax may not be carried back to earlier periods (83).

## HONG KONG

In Hong Kong business enterprises may be organized in several ways, each with differing accounting and reporting responsibilities. Sole proprietorships must be registered with the Inland Revenue Department but are not required to publicly disclose or to have audited financial statements. Liability for single proprietorships is unlimited. In the case of partnerships it may be limited or unlimited. In limited partnerships, one or more general partners who operate the business must have unlimited liability. Specific accounting and auditing rules for partnerships do not exist, but the Partnership Ordinance does require "partners to render true accounts and full information of all matters affecting the partnership" (Byrne 1988, 28).

Foreign corporations may do business in Hong Kong but must register and provide required documentation to the Hong Kong Companies Registrar. Foreign public corporations must provide audited financial statements annually, together with a director's report to the Companies Registrar.

Foreign private corporations are exempted from these reporting requirements.

Companies incorporated in Hong Kong may be organized with limited or unlimited liability. Companies may be private by restricting rights of share transfer and by limiting company shareholders to fifty (Coopers and Lybrand 1991, H-3). A public company may be listed on stock exchanges. Listed companies, many of whom begin as family concerns, must offer a minimum of 25 percent of equity shares to the public. To offer securities to the public, companies must file a proper prospectus with audited financial statements for the preceding five years with the Companies Registrar. Companies whose stock is listed on the stock exchange must comply with Securities (Stock Exchange Listing) Rules and the rules set by the Stock Exchange. Once listed, companies must provide shareholders, the Exchange, and the Commissioner of Securities with annual audited financial statements and interim unaudited financial reports for the first six months of each year. Limited companies must prepare financial statements in accordance with the Companies Ordinance and the Statements of Standard Accounting Practices issued by the Hong Kong Society of Accountants.

The general public may inspect listed company filings for a fee. Interim and final results of company operations must be published in the local newspapers (H-3). Every incorporated firm is required at its annual meeting to appoint an auditor who is a CPA holding a practicing certificate issued by the Hong Kong Society of Accountants (Byrne 1988, 1, 9). The auditor reports whether the company's financial statements "present a true and fair view of the state of affairs of the company, its profit or loss and changes in financial position" (8) and whether the statements "are properly prepared in accordance with the Companies Ordinance" (8).

Public companies must file their audit report and related financial statements with the Companies Registrar on an annual basis. Private companies are exempt from such filings. The Hong Kong Inland Revenue Department requires the audit report and financial statements to be submitted with tax returns (Byrne 1988, 10).

In 1973, the Professional Accountants Ordinance made the Hong Kong Society of Accountants the only official accounting body in Hong Kong. The Society was given the authority to formulate Hong Kong accounting and auditing standards. It was also charged with the responsibility to conduct accountancy examinations, to prescribe the experience deemed necessary for receiving a practice certificate and to keep a register of professional accountants meeting the requirements to serve as such. The Society issues practice certificates annually (Price Waterhouse 1992a, 9).

It also issues a number of pronouncements concerning basic accounting techniques, standards and guidelines. These codifications are based largely upon related statements issued by United Kingdom accounting institutes.

According to Byrne, Hong Kong auditing standards and guidelines "tend to allow more room for professional judgement" (1988, 10) as compared to the more codified United States standards. There are a number of auditing practices followed routinely by Hong Kong auditors for which codified guidelines have not been issued. When an auditor states the opinion that the financial statements present a true and fair picture, the employment of all applicable standard accounting practices is assumed.

Financial statements must comply with the pronouncements set forth by the Society and the Companies Ordinance. Statements of Standard Accounting Practice and Accounting Guidelines are the two series in which the Society codifies accounting practice. Financial statements of nonlisted companies may be in English or Chinese. Those of listed companies must be in English but would generally include a Chinese translation (101).

Various differences exist between generally accepted accounting principles in Hong Kong and the United States. Historical cost is the primary basis of valuation in Hong Kong, but alternative methods are permitted. Revaluations of tangible fixed-asset accounts and related accumulated-depreciation accounts may be made based on a current valuation. Fixed assets may be revalued based upon directors' estimation or valuation. Such departures from historical cost must be disclosed in footnotes (Byrne 1988, 20).

In Hong Kong, land is held on long-term lease and cannot be owned. Leaseholds for land with lease terms of less than fifty years are amortized while those in excess of fifty years are not amortized. There is no standard for disclosing industry segment information for all companies, but an accounting guideline has been issued that is followed by a minority of companies (81).

Subsidiaries are included in consolidated statements except when the business of the subsidiary is dissimilar to that of others in the consolidated entity, when the control of the subsidiary by parent is significantly impaired for the foreseeable future or when control is expected to be temporary. There is no standard for business combination accounting, nor do criteria for the pooling of interest treatment exist.

Goodwill is permitted to be carried as a permanent intangible asset unless its value is permanently impaired. It may also be charged off at the time of acquisition to a reserve account or an extraordinary profit or loss. Or, it may be written off over a defined period of time (21). The predominant practice is to carry goodwill from a business combination as an asset and amortize the total over periods estimated to benefit (79).

Imputed interest is not used for receivables or payables that occurred in transactions not subject to the usual trade terms or outside the usual course of business. Inventory methods are disclosed and must result in the closest practical approximation of actual cost. Thus, while FIFO and average cost are in widespread use, LIFO is not used. There is no requirement concerning research costs or development costs. There are various treatments in use and, unless the size or incidence of the costs are exceptional or extraordinary, disclosures are not made (86).

No accounting standards exist for pensions, and few enterprises have established pension plans for their employees (Byrne 1988, 88). Tax-loss carrybacks are not permitted in Hong Kong. Tax losses are carried forward and reported as reductions of tax expense in the period realized.

# 5

## ACCOUNTING ENVIRONMENTS IN SELECTED EMERGING ASIAN-PACIFIC ECONOMIES

### THE PHILIPPINES

In the Philippines businesses may take the form of single proprietorships, partnerships or corporations. Single proprietorships must register with the Bureau of Domestic Trade and obtain a municipal business license. Partnership law is founded in United States partnership laws, the Uniform Partnership Act and the Limited Partnership Act. Partnerships must have at least one general partner. All general partners are subject to unlimited liability. Partnerships with capital exceeding P3,000 must register with the Security Exchange Commission (SGV and Co. 1989, 25–26).

Books of account must be kept by all taxpayers, whether personal or corporate. Taxpayers with quarterly sales or receipts not exceeding P5,000 may use simplified bookkeeping records authorized by the Secretary of Finance. Books must be approved by the Bureau of Internal Revenue prior to use, and computerized records are generally approved after verification and inspection by a Bureau examiner.

Philippine companies are governed by the Corporation Code, which is comparable to United States corporate law. In some cases special laws or charters may be used to establish a corporation. Corporations may be either private or public. Corporate board members must be stockholders, and a majority must be residents of the Philippines. The board must present a financial report for preceding-year operations, including audited financial statements at a regular stockholder meeting.

Branches of foreign corporations may be established to conduct business in the Philippines. Such firms must obtain licenses from the Security Exchange Commission and must make security deposits. Although no industries are closed to private enterprise, the Omnibus Investments Code of 1987 allows 100 percent foreign ownership of business entities only for specified exporting businesses in which at least 70 percent of production is exported and in firms operating in designated pioneer or less-developed areas. The Foreign Investments Act of 1991 lists areas where foreign ownership is prohibited or restricted to various percentages of total ownership. Permitted percentages range upwards to 40 percent (Price Waterhouse 1993b, 43–53).

Public offerings of securities must be registered with the Philippines Security Exchange Commission, and such registration must be published in two general-circulation newspapers for two consecutive weeks. The registration statement must be accompanied by a corporate balance sheet dated no more than 90 days before filing and by income statements for the prior three years. The financial statements must be audited by an independent certified public accountant (SGV and Co. 1989, 26).

The nation has two stock exchanges, Manila and Makati. Listing requirements for both are similar and include the filing with the exchange of the latest audited financial statements when the application for listing is made and when financial statements are submitted to the stockholders. An application for listing on the exchange must be approved by the Security Exchange Commission.

Companies with capital of P50,000 or more must file audited financial statements with the Security Exchange Commission. If corporate gross quarterly sales exceed P25,000, audited financial statements must be filed with income tax returns to the Bureau of Internal Revenue. Filings with the Security Exchange Commission are normally open to the public. Auditors must be independent certified public accountants. They are selected by company management, which may need approval of the stockholders or board of directors. Company managements hold primary responsibilities for maintaining proper records and books of account.

The accounting profession in the Philippines is governed by the Revised Accountancy Law of 1975 (SGV and Co. 1989, 1). The title of certified public accountant requires a valid certificate of registration from the Board of Accountancy, which is supervised by the Professional Regulation Commission. The Commission recognizes the Philippine Institute of Certified Public Accountants as the official CPA organization. Various other accounting organizations exist that may be joined by holders of valid CPA certificates. In 1988 membership in the Institute stood at 25,000, with an estimated 26 percent in public practice, 18 percent in government service, 39 percent in commerce and industry, 10 percent in education and 7 percent in other lines of work (6).

To obtain a certificate of registration, accountants must pass an examination and be citizens of at least 21 years of age. They must be of good character and must hold a Bachelor of Science in Commerce or its equivalent from a college recognized by the government. Reciprocity is extended to CPAs from countries that extend a similar courtesy.

Audit standards are set by the Auditing Standards and Practice Council, which was formed in 1986. After approval by the Board of Accountancy and the Professional Regulation Commission, the audit standards are mandatory for all CPAs. Accountants may practice as single proprietors or in partnership arrangements. Incorporation is not permitted (5). Continuing professional education is a condition for the renewal of the CPA certificate.

Although the generally accepted auditing standards are similar to the United States standards that were in effect prior to 1988, there are a substantial number of differences between required audit practices in the Philippines and the United States. Often these differences are in the promulgated official audit procedures, while in practice most CPAs carry out procedures similar to United States requirements (49–53).

The confirmation of receivables directly with debtors, although not required, is the predominant practice. Similarly, the observation of physical inventory-taking is not required but nonetheless is the predominant practice (11). The auditor's duties and responsibilities for planning the audit to detect material illegal acts by clients, not to mention errors or irregularities, has not been addressed (12). There are no requirements for the review of subsequent events. In practice most CPAs do perform procedures to identify and report events subsequent to the balance sheet date, which may need adjusting or reporting (12).

The standard audit report is the same as the standard United States two-paragraph report issued prior to 1988. Standards and procedures for departure from the standard report are also similar to those in effect in the United States prior to 1988 (13). Accounting standards are codified by the Accounting Standards Council of the Philippine Institute of Certified Public Accountants. The council first issues exposure drafts and after public comment issues statements of Financial Accounting Standards. After approval by the Board of Accountancy and the Professional Regulation Commission these standards become part of the rules and regulations governing CPAs.

Statements of Financial Accounting Standards are said to be "influenced" in large measure by United States accounting principles, yet there are significant differences not only in requirements but also in the predominant practices being followed (16). Consolidated financial statements are not required, nor is it the predominant practice to issue consolidated reports if not required by a governmental agency (16).

The revaluation of property, plant and equipment by a change to stockholders' equity is permitted based on index numbers or on independent appraisal. However, no suitable index numbers have been assigned for the purpose of revaluation (17). In other words, revaluations have been based on independent appraisals.

Disclosure of segmental operations is not required, nor is it a predominant practice. Operating losses may not be carried back to prior years. There are no requirements related to Statements of Financial Accounting Standards in a large number of other areas where the predominant practice is nevertheless carried out in the Philippines by practices similar to those in the United States. Among such practices are the capitalization of interest costs on construction projects, accounting for nonmonetary assets at fair market value, accounting for business combinations, asset reporting by current or noncurrent classes, interest imputed on receivables and payables, lease accounting, accounting for long-term construction, contracts, research and development costs, pension cost accounting, deferred income taxes and gains and losses on foreign currency transactions (54–71).

## INDONESIA

Indonesian company law is based on the Commerce Code and the Civil Code of 1847. Modeled on Dutch laws of the colonial era, the commercial laws of Indonesia have not kept abreast of subsequent changes in Dutch law. Nonetheless, many modern Dutch provisos are common practice in Indonesia. For example although the Commercial Code contains no provisions for limited liability, notaries public include them in the articles of incorporation as companies are established. These are legally binding and have the same effect as law. Notaries public in Indonesia are appointed by the Minister of Justice and are considered a part of the legal profession. They act as legal agents for a variety of activities including the preparation of articles of incorporation that establish a limited liability company. Company law is in the process of revision, but the Indonesian Parliament has yet to enact the revisions.

Commerce may be undertaken by Indonesians through sole proprietorships or partnerships. Noncitizens cannot engage in either form of business. Partnerships are of three types. The basic partnership customarily used for professional entities such as lawyers, notaries and accountants is formed by a contractual agreement without official filing or governmental approval and need not be disclosed to third parties. A disclosed partnership is used to hold a business name and is used customarily by trading and service entities. As this is a form of the basic partnership, basic partnership rules apply (Price Waterhouse 1993a, 98).

Limited partnerships consist of one or more active partners and one or more silent partners. The active partner, who may manage the entity, is liable for the entire debt of the partnership. The silent partner, who may not perform managerial functions, is liable only to the extent of partnership contributions. This form is an extension of the disclosed partnership and must meet all requirements of a disclosed partnership (98).

Foreign investment is under government control. Such investments are generally in the form of joint ventures with domestic participation required. Joint ventures frequently take the form of limited liability companies, in which the joint participants are the shareholders. Joint ventures may take the form of either private or public companies. At their inception generally 20 percent of the equity must be owned by locals. The percentage of Indonesian ownership must be increased to 51 percent within twenty years. However, there are exceptions to and variations on the rules for required Indonesian ownership (89).

Branches of foreign corporations may be established in exceptional cases and must be registered with relevant ministries. Such entities may have a representative office for promotional, quality control or procurement activities but may not engage in business activities. None has been established in recent years.

Companies may be listed on the Jakarta or Surabaya Stock Exchanges or in the over-the-counter market, regulated by the Capital Market Executive Board. The markets have similar listing requirements except that the list mentioned is somewhat less stringent on required years of operation and size of investment. Listed companies must be registered in Indonesia and have limited liability. They must submit audited financial statements that received an unqualified audit opinion for the year prior to listing.

Financial reporting for public companies is still developing. However, the chairman of the Capital Market Executive Board has issued *Guidelines on the Format and Contents of a Financial Report*. These apply to public companies and extend accounting and reporting standards (Coopers and

Lybrand 1992, I-2). A majority of the trade company shares must be owned by Indonesians (Price Waterhouse 1993a, 63).

The Commercial Code envisions that annual financial statements be presented at annual general company meetings, but there is no overall audit requirement (Coopers and Lybrand 1992, I-2). Publicly held corporations must have a statutory audit. Other companies must have audited accounts for most foreign investment entities in their contract of work or, if called for, in their articles of incorporation. Income tax authorities do not require audited accounts with their tax returns (Price Waterhouse 1993a, 115).

Audits must be performed by public accountants registered with the Indonesian Association of Accountants. That body, which regulates accountants in the nation, has 11,500 members, one-half of whom are estimated to be in government service. Until recently a three-year term of government service was required of graduates from accounting programs, which was perceived to be causing a severe shortage of accountants in the private sector. The Association's influence does not compare to that of similar bodies in Western nations. However, it is continuing to develop. Indonesian firms provide accounting, auditing, taxation, and management advisory services and act as correspondents for their international accounting counterparts (115).

The Indonesian Association of Accountants publishes generally accepted auditing standards. These were issued first in 1974 and underwent a major revision in 1984. These have been based in large measure upon United States standards. Government-owned companies are audited by government auditors who follow audit standards set by the government. These standards differ substantially in nature and objectives from those in the private sector (116).

In Indonesia accounting practices are frequently preferred rather than prescribed. Alternative accounting practices that comply with general principles or practices are commonly used. Generally accepted accounting principles (GAAP) for Indonesia are codified in Indonesian Accounting Principles, Statements on Accounting Standards and Interpretations of Indonesian Accounting Principles issued by the Steering Committee of the Indonesian Accountants Association but remain incomplete in comprehensiveness and precision. The main principles, which as indicated earlier were updated in 1984, have been supplemented periodically in accounting statements and interpretations on specific issues. Public companies are also required to follow the Capital Market Executive Board Circular attachment, which sets guidelines on the format and contents of a financial report and extends requirements in a number of areas beyond those generally required in Indonesian GAAP.

The fundamental concepts for Indonesian GAAP are based on the American Institute of Certified Public Accountants' 1965 publication *Accounting Research Study No. 7: Inventory of Generally Accepted Accounting Principles for Business Enterprises*. Later developments in accounting principles in developed countries have in part been incorporated into Indonesian GAAP (119). The International Accounting Standards issued by the International Accounting Standards Committee may also be used (Coopers and Lybrand 1992, I-1).

Some specific areas in which Indonesian GAAP differ from United States GAAP are important to consider. The statement of changes in financial position may be prepared using either cash or net working capital as a basis. Public companies only are required to report earnings per share, but details of computations are not codified. Public companies only have a requirement for accounting treatment for discontinued operations to be separately reported. There are no requirements for segmental information on either a line of business or geographical basis. Segment information is generally not reported (I-7).

Consolidated financial statements are rare. In practice, consolidation is treated as not mandatory, and many subsidiaries are not consolidated. Thus minority interests are not reported. Either the equity or the cost method may be used to account for unconsolidated subsidiaries, although the equity method is preferred where the parent has significant control of the investee.

Detailed guidance is not provided for business affiliations. Goodwill arising from a purchase of a business is treated as having an unlimited life. Details of goodwill computations are not included in pronouncements. The treatment of pension costs has not been addressed in GAAP, and costs are generally accounted for on a cash basis.

Imputed interest is not considered in Indonesian GAAP. Liabilities are recorded at "the monetary value assigned to the economic sacrifice that will be incurred upon settlement of the obligation at the future due date" (I-12). Guidance for the accounting treatment of related party transactions is generally lacking (I-7). Tangible fixed assets may be revalued when permitted by government authority. Revaluations have been made previously only for devaluations of the rupiah (I-8). Depreciation methods approved are the straight-line and declining-balance methods.

Research costs are not addressed as such in Indonesian GAAP and are given the same treatment as any other intangible asset. That is, they may be considered to have a limited life with expense charges made over the asset's useful life or to have an unlimited life, in which case "the rate of amortization should be based on reasonable judgment" (I-8).

Income tax expense is generally recorded at the amount of current taxes payable with no provisions for deferred taxation. Provisions may be made for timing differences between taxable and accounting income using liability methods. Tax loss may not be carried back but may be carried forward for up to five years. Once financial statements have been issued, there is no requirement for retroactive restatement in the event of subsequent discovery of accounting errors that affect prior periods.

In Malaysia business and commercial activities may be carried out through a sole proprietorship or in partnership, registered in accordance with the Business Registration Act. The latter format carries unlimited liability. Partnerships may be formed by individuals or corporations. If business for gain is the purpose of the partnership, no more than twenty partners are permitted. Partners are, in general, jointly liable for partnership obligations, and each partner is personally liable for obligations not settled by the partnership (Price Waterhouse 1994b, 90).

Joint ventures may be carried out by partnerships or may be incorporated. A company registered outside Malaysia may establish a branch with prior approval of the Ministry of Trade and Industry, which is reluctant generally to register branches except for specific projects (90).

Beyond government enterprises, business is conducted primarily by private or public companies incorporated under the Companies Act of 1965. In general such companies have liability limited to amounts paid for shares. A private company may have no more than fifty shareholders, must restrict transfer rights of shares and must not invite public subscription for shares, debentures or deposit of money. Private companies with no more than twenty shareholders or beneficial ownership by another corporation can qualify as exempt private companies, which exempts them from filing annual accounting reports with the Company Registry where public inspection is available (78–80).

A company must not deal in its own shares. The company secretary, who is viewed as primarily responsible for compliance with company law, and at least two members of the board of directors must have principal residence in Malaysia (84). Each company must keep accounting books and other records such that a true and fair report can be prepared for its operations. Records and books for Malaysian operations must be kept in Malaysia. Audited financial statements and other required information must be filed with the Registrar of Companies and with the tax authorities each year by all but exempt private companies. Each company incorporated under the

Companies Act is required to have shareholders appoint company auditors at the annual meeting. These auditors must be independent and must be approved by the Minister of Finance. They must be members of the Malaysian Institute of Accountants, must be Malaysian citizens and must have principal residence in Malaysia.

The Malaysian Institute of Accountants, established by the Accountants' Act of 1967, is charged with the regulation of the accounting profession in Malaysia. Members of other accountancy bodies such as the Malaysian Association of Certified Public Accountants may become members. The latter organization conducts accountancy examinations in Malaysia (105–106).

In practice the two organizations mentioned above jointly oversee accounting and auditing practices in the nation. They approve the International Auditing Practices Committee's International Auditing Guidelines and the International Accounting Standards Committee's International Accounting Standards deemed appropriate for operation in Malaysia. As needed they also issue Malaysian Auditing Guidelines and Malaysian Accounting Standards (108). These guidelines and standards and the approved international standards form Malaysian generally accepted auditing and accounting standards with which company accounts and audits must comply.

Approving international standards for Malaysian operations involves a time lag. In a few cases the Malaysian Institute of Accountants and the Malaysian Association of Certified Public Accountants determine that separate Malaysian Accounting Standards would be more appropriate than the international pronouncement (110). Overall it seems as though generally accepted accounting principles as applied in Malaysia compare quite favorably with those of the United States.

## THAILAND

In Thailand business organizations may take the form of limited liability companies, partnerships, joint ventures or branches of foreign corporations. Partnerships may be unregistered ordinary partnerships in which partners are jointly and indefinitely liable for total partnership debt, registered ordinary partnerships whose partner's liability is limited to two years after leaving the partnership and limited partnerships that may have nonmanaging partners with liability limited to contributions but must have at least one fully liable managing partner (Ernst and Young 1990, 19–20).

Joint ventures are not recognized as legal entities in Thailand under the Civil and Commercial Code but may be used for tax declaration purposes.

Branches of foreign corporations must have approval to be established (20). Both domestic and foreign business interests favor the limited liability company form over other alternatives. Limited liability companies are provided for in the Civil and Commercial Code (private companies) or under the Public Companies Act of 1978 (public companies). Public companies face severe ownership restrictions. They require more than 100 shareholders, with at least 50 percent of the stock held by small shareholders each holding no more than 0.6 percent of the total stock. No more than 10 percent of the stock of a public company can be held by one entity. A private company must have at least seven shareholders. While public company shareholders must pay for securities in full, those of private companies may make partial payment (25 percent of the share par value). Faced with such restrictions, private companies are reluctant to adopt the public form of ownership. The ownership requirements for public companies are in the process of being changed.

The Securities Exchange of Thailand is organized as a nonprofit entity and acts as both a market for securities and a regulatory agency. Companies are encouraged to be listed through the use of tax incentives (8). Accounting books and related records must be kept by every company at its registered office. Such records must generally be kept on file for ten years. All companies must be audited annually by a licensed independent auditor. Audited annual financial statements once approved at the annual stockholders meeting must be filed with the Ministry of Commerce. The statements must also accompany the annual income tax returns to the Revenue Department.

Licensed auditors are governed by the Institute of Certified Accountants and Auditors of Thailand and the Board of Supervision of Auditing Practice. The Institute, an independent professional entity formed in 1948, issues proposals for generally accepted auditing standards, which must be approved by the Board of Supervision of Auditing Practice. As of 1991, thirty-one auditing standards had been issued. The standards have been based largely upon similar United States standards (Akathaporn et al. 1993, 261). The Board, which is an agency of the Ministry of Commerce, is responsible for controlling the audit profession (261). It issues practice licenses to qualified auditors and may cancel those licenses for cause.

Although Thailand's economy has been experiencing substantial expansion, there is an acute shortage of qualified accountants (260). To qualify for an audit license an applicant must pass an examination given by the board. Applicants for the examination must hold "a baccalaureate degree with an adequate number of accounting courses" (261). The applicant must be a citizen, at least twenty years of age, with at least 2,000 hours of public accounting experience in the preceding two years. All parts of the examination must be passed in one sitting. The licensed auditor is expected to uphold the 1968 Code of Ethics.

If the practitioner does not audit at least five companies per year, a series of seminars offered by the Institute of Certified Accountants and Auditors of Thailand must be attended to maintain the audit license (261). The Institute has the responsibility for setting accounting standards. As of 1990, sixteen standards were issued. They tend to follow International Accounting Standards or United States generally accepted accounting principles. In the absence of local standards, International or United States standards may be used. "The general trend is to follow the International Accounting Standards" (Ernst and Young 1990, 3).

Financial statements may consist of only the balance sheet and income statement unless the reporting firm is listed on the Securities Exchange of Thailand or is a financial institution, in which case the statement of changes in financial positions is required.

Although investment by foreign interests is encouraged, some areas are restricted. Domestic ownership must surpass 50 percent in many business and professional service pursuits unless permission is obtained from the Ministry of Commerce. Such permissions are seldom granted. A bilateral treaty between Thailand and the United States (the Treaty of Amity and Economic Relations) permits United States corporations to have wholly owned subsidiaries or branches with few restrictions on investment (13). Although ownership rights for foreigners are restricted, foreign nationals may manage and control companies through minority ownership. Foreigners wishing to work in Thailand must obtain long-term visa status and work permits. Such individuals may find language an added restriction.

# 6

# THE CLIMATE FOR ACCOUNTING AMONG THE PACIFIC ISLAND ECONOMIES

As in the case of the Asian Tigers and the emerging nations of the Pacific, the island economies have developed various domestic laws and institutions that impact business procedures and the service needs of firms of various types. The accounting profession in those island jurisdictions is affected by those institutional constraints and procedures in at least two ways. Accountants are needed for preparing various reports and documents called for by the laws of the jurisdictions concerned, and in addition most jurisdictions have laws or procedures governing membership in the accounting profession. In this chapter the institutional climates of certain island economies will be reviewed. It was thought that a detailed discussion of each and every island jurisdiction might prove cumbersome. Instead, selected economies will be highlighted. Those chosen include Fiji, Western Samoa, Vanuatu and Papua New Guinea.

## FIJI

Business enterprises in Fiji may take the form of sole proprietorship, partnership, branch of a foreign company or corporate entity. Proprietorships and partnerships need not be registered with the Registrar of Companies unless the business name differs from the names of the individuals doing business. The Partnership Act does not provide for limited liability partnerships. Joint ventures generally take on the characteristics, including the legal rights and responsibilities, of either partnership or corporation (Price Waterhouse 1994a, 50–51).

The Companies Act governs Fiji corporations and branches of foreign companies operating in Fiji and is patterned on United Kingdom Companies Acts, with some modifications that allow for local conditions. Articles of incorporation and related documentation must be filed with the Registrar of Companies. Companies may have legal liability that is unlimited, limited to shares or limited to amounts guaranteed. Virtually all companies are formed with liability limited to shares. The name of a limited liability company must contain the word "limited" (46).

Private companies may be formed with two to fifty shareholders with restricted rights of share transfer. Securities may not be publicly sold. Such private companies are not required to file annual financial statements with the Registrar of Companies.

Public companies must have at least seven shareholders. A prospectus must be filed with the Registrar of Companies for public issuance of securities. Shares in a public company may be freely transferred, but Exchange Control approval is needed for shares to be owned by foreigners (48). At least two directors of a public company must reside in Fiji, one for a private company. A company secretary resident in Fiji is generally required.

An annual general stockholders' meeting is required at which directors present the company income statement and balance sheet accompanied by a directors' report and an auditor's report if made. Public companies must appoint an auditor who holds a certificate of public practice from the Fiji Institute of Accountants (FIA). Audits are not a requirement for a private company when at the annual company meeting all shareholders unanimously resolve that an auditor not be appointed. Despite such a resolution by a private company, the Registrar of Companies may still require that an auditor be appointed. When the company does not have an auditor, the balance sheet of the private company must include a statement that the accounts are unaudited (63).

Foreign corporations must register with the Registrar of Companies, providing detailed company information. The foreign company's annual financial statements for the company as a whole must be filed as required for local companies. A separate statement for operations in Fiji is not required. The foreign company operating in Fiji must publicly display its name, country of incorporation and whether shareholders have limited liability (54).

All companies must keep books of account and other records in English sufficient to prepare financial statements that give a true and fair view of company operations and financial conditions. Copies of the audited financial statements must be filed with the Registrar of Companies by public companies. Private companies as noted above are exempt from this filing. Companies listed on the Fiji Stock Exchange are required to distribute annual financial statements to all shareholders. Although usually provided where available, audited financial statements are not required to be filed with tax authorities.

Duties of the auditor contained in the Companies Act of 1983 include reporting to shareholders an audit opinion on financial statements and whether information required by the Companies Act is properly given by the accounts. Specific procedures and practices to be followed by the auditor are not contained in the legislation.

The Fiji Institute of Accountants (FIA) was formed in 1972 to improve accountancy in Fiji. Membership is available to those with approved overseas qualifications and to local accountants who have received the appropriate degree from the University of the South Pacific in Suva and have the prerequisite practical experience. For public practice of accountancy a certificate of practice in Fiji is required (64).

The FIA issues accounting standards and statements of auditing practice. These are contained in the FIA handbook for its members. Where the FIA has not issued standards, accountants may follow international accounting standards and standards of the United Kingdom, Australia and New Zealand (64). Fiji's auditing practice standards are comparable to the International Auditing Standards (65).

The auditor's report indicates that Fiji auditing standards were followed and presents the auditor's opinion on the true and fair view given by the financial statements and books of account. The report also indicates whether information requirements of the Companies Act of 1983 were adhered to (65).

Differences of note between the Fiji accounting standards and those of the U.S. are several. Marketable securities may be valued at market when lower than cost, at the discretion of the directors. The last-in-first-out (LIFO) inventory method is not permitted. Real property held as fixed assets may be valued upward to market value with the increment charged to a revaluation reserve. Machinery and equipment may be revalued upward from cost by directors' or independent appraisal. The diminishing-balance method of depreciation is permitted. Investment tax credits are taken to current income in the year received. Goodwill on purchase of another company need not be written off against revenue over its life, but this practice is becoming more common. The pooling-of-interests method of company affiliations is not used. Interperiod income tax allocation for timing differences is not required (70–72).

## WESTERN SAMOA

Business entities in Western Samoa may be sole proprietorships, partnerships or companies. Although the business name of proprietorships and partnerships does not have to be registered, a business license must be obtained from the Department of Economic Affairs by all business organizations. All forms of business are open to domestic and foreign investors.

The Western Samoa Partnership Act of 1975, which governs partnerships, requires that no more than twenty-five partners may be included in any partnership except for professional partnerships, which may have up to fifty members. Anyone can enter into a partnership with any other person without restriction as to nationality or residency. Partners have joint liability for partnership obligations. The limited liability form of partnership is not provided in the statute, although the same ends can be accomplished in the partnership agreement where all partners agree that some partners will have limited liability (Price Waterhouse 1991b, 29).

Company law in Samoa consists of the Samoa Companies Order of 1935. Although most companies have liability limited by shares, corporations may be formed that have unlimited liability or liability limited by guarantee (25).

Companies may be public or private. A private company may have between two and twenty-five stockholders and may not sell shares to the public. Shareholders are not required to be nationals or resident in Western Samoa. No restrictions exist that would prohibit another company from holding shares through a nominee shareholder. Foreign purchase of shares is not restricted by exchange controls (27). Public offerings of securities require that a prospectus be filed with the Registrar of Companies. Western Samoa does not have a securities market.

Public companies must have a minimum of seven shareholders. Each company must have a secretary and, for private companies, at least one director. At least two directors are required for a public company. Secretaries and directors need not be resident in Western Samoa (26).

A branch of a foreign corporation may conduct business in Western Samoa by providing the Registrar of Companies with the company's articles of incorporation and bylaws and names of company directors and secretary and by designating a resident in Western Samoa as authorized to accept company legal and other notices. Branches must keep accounting and other records and make the same annual filings with the Registrar as do Western Samoan public companies. Foreign corporations operating in Western Samoa must also display in appropriate ways the company name and country of incorporation and whether they have limited liability status (28).

The Companies Ordinance requires that accounting and related records be kept at each company's registered office such that a report can be made to the Registrar of Companies each year. The report must contain a summary of share capital, details of indebtedness, and a list of shareholders with details of shares transferred, among other information. Financial statements are required to accompany this report only for public companies.

Public companies must also present audited annual financial statements to stockholders at the annual meeting. Accordingly, all public companies in Western Samoa must appoint an auditor at the company's annual general meeting. Private companies are not required to appoint an auditor, but many do. Entities using other forms of business do not have these requirements for audited accounts (35).

Appointed auditors must be registered under the provisions of the Samoan Companies Order of 1935. The Western Samoan Society of Accountants (WSSA) was formed in 1959. Individuals who have the qualifications adopted by the WSSA are known as Certified Public Accountants. Samoan auditors follow international auditing guidelines in conducting examinations of accounts and financial statements (36).

Western Samoa has adopted the accounting principles of the International Accounting Standards Committee (36). Some accounting practices specific to Samoa are generally followed. The use of LIFO is not permitted in Western Samoa. Real property may be revalued to reflect inflation. Plant and machinery are depreciated using the diminishing-value method. Depreciation on buildings is not allowable for tax purposes. A number of local companies have adopted depreciation methods and rates applicable for tax purposes (38).

Finally, footnotes to Samoan financial statements usually make disclosures of accounting policies in use, details of capital commitments or contingent liabilities and other material items affecting financial results and position (38).

## VANUATU

English common law is followed in the Vanuatu legal system. Company law is also based on the English system, with the Companies Act patterned after United Kingdom company legislation of 1967 amended to meet local conditions (39). Although there are some forty languages in everyday use, English and French are widely used in business (3).

Forms of business entity that are permitted are sole proprietorships, trusts, partnerships, joint ventures and companies (Price Waterhouse 1992d, 37). Proprietorships and partnerships in Vanuatu have unlimited liability and need not be registered unless the business name differs from that of the proprietor or partners, in which case the Business Names Act requires registration with the Registrar of Companies (42).

Joint ventures may be carried on in any of the other forms of business and must comply with the appropriate regulations for the selected form of business. Trusts under which asset legal ownership is transferred by means of a deed to a trustee for the benefit of trust beneficiaries are used to carry on activities of a financial and business nature. In Vanuatu trusts deeds are not filed with the government, nor are reports on trust administration required (45).

Before a company may begin operations a business license must be issued by the Minister of Finance. The Companies Act permits formation and registration of three classes of companies: local, overseas, and exempted. A local company may carry on business in Vanuatu after receiving a business license from the Minister of Finance. As returns and other materials filed with the Registrar of Companies are available to the public, a local company's beneficial owners can be divulged.

An overseas company is similar to a local company but is incorporated outside of Vanuatu and must apply to the Minister of Finance for a permit to be registered as an overseas company. The articles of incorporation and related materials must be filed by the overseas company when applying. At least two natural persons resident in Vanuatu must be authorized as agents of the company in Vanuatu (38). An overseas company is not required to have an audit but must file annual accounts with the Registrar of Companies (42).

An exempted company must carry on all business activities of the company outside Vanuatu, but such activities may be carried out from within Vanuatu. An exempted company must have a registered office in Vanuatu and have at least two shareholders, a director and a secretary. One meeting of the company per year must be held in Vanuatu. None of the exempted companies' filings or official documentation is publicly available. The public is also barred from any court proceedings involving company affairs. The exempted company must file an annual return with the Registrar, but there are no audit requirements (39).

Companies may be public or private. A private company may have between two and fifty shareholders except when wholly owned by a public company, in which case only one shareholder is required. At least seven shareholders are required for a public company. Each public company must have at least two directors, one for a private company.

The Companies Act requires that accounting and related records be kept for all companies such that true and fair financial statements can be prepared. The records should normally be kept at the company's registered office. Auditors are required to be appointed at the shareholders' annual meeting for all local public companies and for local private companies whose sales exceed VT2 million. Companies, including exempt companies that hold a license under the banking, trust, or insurance regulations, must also appoint an auditor (40).

The auditor of a local company must have a valid business license issued under the Business Licenses Act. There are no Vanuatu auditing standards prescribed. Auditors tend to follow the International Auditing Guidelines. Nor is there a professional or other group that sets accounting standards in Vanuatu. As long as the requirements of the Companies Act are met and in the absence of other requirements, the accounting standards applied will generally be those of the country whose auditing standards are being used.

The accountants engaged in public practice in Vanuatu are members of either the Institute of Chartered Accountants in Australia or the New Zealand Society of Accountants. Therefore, the keeping of accounts and the financial statements in Vanuatu, as long as the requirements of the Companies Act are met, tend to follow the accounting requirements of either of these national bodies. The Australian Institute is dominant. In the absence of other requirements the pronouncements of the International Accounting Standards Committee are generally followed (52).

## PAPUA NEW GUINEA

In Papua New Guinea the types of organizations typically found in other countries are used by business and commerce. Individuals may operate as sole proprietorships. Partnerships of between two and twenty persons, except for professional partnerships, which may not exceed fifty persons, are governed by provisions of the Partnerships Act, the Business Names Act and the Companies Act. Partners are liable for all debts and obligations of the partnership incurred while a partner. Business names if different from the names of the persons in the partnership or sole proprietorship must be registered with the Registrar of Companies. A resident agent is required for each business. Joint ventures may take the form of either partnership or corporation and are subject to the appropriate rules and responsibilities (Price Waterhouse 1990b, 49–59).

Under the Companies Act, corporations may be formed with liability unlimited, limited by shares, by guarantee, by both shares and guarantee, or in the case of mining companies no liability (50). A company that has limited liability is required to have a corporate name that includes *Limited* or *Ltd.* at the end. The most common form of incorporation is liability limited by shares.

To form a corporation, a memorandum of association, or charter, setting forth company particulars must be filed with the Registrar of Companies who issues a certificate of incorporation. To offer shares or debentures to the public, a proper prospectus must also be filed with the Registrar. Filings with the Registrar of Companies are open to public use (51). There is no securities market in the country. Some Papua New Guinea companies are listed on the Australian Stock Exchange (36).

Companies may be public, for which at least three directors must be appointed, or proprietary (private), for which one director is required. There must be at least two directors for a public company, one for a proprietary company, who are natural persons resident in Papua New Guinea. Each company must appoint a secretary who normally will be resident in Papua New Guinea and present during normal office hours at the registered office of the company (52). A company may not deal in its own shares or in a parent company's shares. However, financial assistance may be provided to a trustee for shares that will benefit employees (46).

All companies must have an annual meeting of stockholders at which the directors' report, a statement of accounts and appointment of an auditor, are included. An exempt proprietary company is not required to appoint an auditor if all shareholders agree not to do so. Company auditors are required to make their reports as set forth in the Companies Act (53).

A branch of a company incorporated in a foreign country may operate in Papua New Guinea but must file documents of registration with the Registrar of Companies. The foreign company must have a resident registered agent who is personally responsible for compliance with the Companies Act. If the company has limited liability, adequate and proper public notice must be given, with *Limited* or *Ltd.* at the end of the company name. An annual return must be filed with the Registrar, reporting current particulars of the company, as well as for foreign public companies, a copy of the annual corporate balance sheet for the entire foreign company as it is prepared under the laws and requirements of its country of incorporation. Should the country of origin not require a corporate balance sheet, one must be prepared and filed in accordance with the requirements for public companies incorporated in Papua New Guinea. Foreign corporations, which are essentially the same as a proprietary company in Papua New Guinea, are not required to file the annual balance sheet. Company law has no requirements for the keeping of branch records except for tax purposes, nor is the foreign corporation branch required to be audited (54–58).

The Companies Act requires all companies incorporated in Papua New Guinea to keep accounting and related records in English that will adequately explain company transactions and financial position. These records are normally kept at the registered office of the corporation and must allow the proper preparation of financial statements that report the results of company operations and financial position (65). The company auditor reports to shareholders whether or not the statements of accounts present a true and fair picture and comply with the provisions of the Companies Act. A copy of the financial statements and audit report must be filed with the Registrar (42).

By Act of Parliament in 1974 the Accountants Registration Board of Papua New Guinea (Board) was instituted, with its primary responsibility being to register qualified accountants, to set qualifications for registry, to regulate accounting practice and to investigate the activities of registered accountants. All persons who practice accounting for a fee must be properly registered with the Board (66).

The Board has the power to set audit, accounting and ethical standards where not included in the Companies Act, but it has not done so. The Papua New Guinea Association of Accountants (PNGAA) was formed with membership from "suitably qualified Papua New Guineans and expatriates" (66) in order to promote the interest of accounting professionals. The PNGAA has not issued guidance on auditing practices and standards. The international accounting firms in Papua New Guinea have in practice used the auditing and ethical standards set by the International Auditing Guidelines. The audit report consists of the statement of opinion by the auditor as to whether the financial statements and the books and related records comply with the Companies Act and whether the financial statements present a true and fair reporting of Company affairs and results (67).

The PNGAA has adopted seventeen Accounting Standards that its members are required to observe. Departures from the promulgations should be disclosed and if not justified may result in a qualified opinion about the true and fair presentation. Two standards were prepared and issued locally: PNGAS1, "Profit and loss statement," and PNGAS2, "Materiality in financial statements." The remaining fifteen are international standards that the PNGAA considered relevant to local conditions. These are approximately half of the current international standards now in force (67).

Differences between standard reporting in Papua New Guinea and the U.S. include the provision that all income and expense, whether relating to prior periods or not, accounting errors or the like, are included in net profit of the period. Extraordinary items in the operating statement include disposal or sale of a major business segment, gains or losses caused by major currency realignment and sale of an investment not acquired for resale. Where marketable securites value is below current market price, adjustment is made at the discretion of the directors. The last-in-first-out inventory method is not permitted. The direct-costing method may be used for inventory. When real property is held for resale, it is treated as a composite asset upon which no depreciation is taken. If real property is not held for resale, an increase in value above cost may be booked in the asset account with the offset to a revaluation reserve. Machinery and equipment may include a directors' or independently determined revaluation amount in addition to cost. Investment tax credits given as investment incentives are charged to income in the period received (71, 72).

Pooling is not a recognized method for affiliating companies. Unconsolidated affiliated company investment may be carried at either the equity or cost method. December 31 must be used as year end for tax purposes. This is commonly followed for financial reporting, but other accounting periods may be adopted (75).

# PART III

## THE MAJOR ACCOUNTING FIRMS AND REGIONAL DEVELOPMENTAL CONCERNS

# 7

## THE ROLE OF THE FIRMS IN SELECTED NEWLY INDUSTRIALIZED ASIAN ECONOMIES

Certainly the impressive growth records of the economies categorized as the "Asian Tigers" can be attributed to manufacturing for export. Together, Hong Kong, Taiwan, Singapore and South Korea were producing a gross national product of $200 billion by the mid-1980s, and that figure was growing at the rate of about 10 percent per year (Kelly and London 1989, 19). "Their combined trade surplus with the United States was about $30 billion" (19). Indeed, a businessman was quoted as saying that "These countries aren't just super economies," rather, "they are like engines pulling a whole region that easily takes in more than 200 million people before you count China" (19).

Employment gains experienced by the economies in question have been described as "the predictable consequences of the expansion of labor-intensive manufactured exports" (Islam and Kirkpatrick 1986, 113). Islam and Kirkpatrick suggested that "The employment intensity of the export-oriented industrialization (EOI) strategy is in turn seen as the major factor behind improvements in income distribution" (113). Those authors point out that, with the possible exception of Hong Kong, the outward-looking industrialization of the economies in question was accompanied by "widespread government intervention and control with the visible arm of the state being more evident than the invisible hand of the market" (114).

In many Third World nations that are oriented towards free enterprise there is no doubt that the government or, more specifically, public planning authorities have more to do with the economy than most wealthier capitalistic jurisdictions might accept. Islam and Kirkpatrick are no doubt correct in observing that "The economic success of the Asian NICs has been based on extensive intervention and economic management by the state" (125).

Judgments concerning the political tactics used or the specifics of how such interventions have impacted local populations in the short run lie beyond the parameters of this book, which is concerned with the realities of the international linkages that have developed. More specifically, it is concerned with how those linkages have spanned the Pacific and how they may be affecting the relations of the jurisdictions in question with other Far Eastern nations, not to mention how they are forging international, yet regional linkages in that part of the globe. It is hoped that an examination of services and in particular the role of the international accounting firms will add to an understanding of the issues involved as they pertain to the economies under discussion in this chapter.

Although trade with the United States has been significant in the growth of the four economies in question, it may be that regional trade or at least trade with other Asian nations may be more important to those jurisdictions in the future. Commenting on Korean prospects, Kihwan Kim has suggested that that nation "is in a good position to exploit the economic dynamism of the Pacific Basin, particularly by expanding its economic relations with its two giant neighbors, Japan and China" (1988, 9). Kim was correct in noting that an export-oriented growth strategy has generated a substantial spatial and sectoral redistribution of income (10). In effect, such a strategy, where adopted, invariably realigns the economy in favor of export sectors. Even where governments have no direct involvement in the production of export goods, they will undoubtedly slant the infrastructure toward export activity. In the case of Korea, Kim has reported that "By its nature the outward-looking development strategy favors the concentration of economic activities in areas which enjoy good transportation networks and natural harbors" (10).

Economists have known for some time the impact that multinational firms can have on the infrastructures of economies that host their facilities (Parry 1973). Even in jurisdictions where production for export is in the hands of domestic interests, infrastructures can be slanted in the direction of those exports. In cases where the entire growth strategies of economies have been based upon exports, major domestic impacts are hardly surprising. Activities that reinforce exports will emerge and will position themselves so as best to perform that function. Decisions by planning authorities to base growth and perhaps development upon exports accept implicitly that the economies in question will adopt an external slant.

Writing in 1984, Larry E. Westphal and his colleagues suggested that "under Korea's strategy of export-led industrialization, export activity has been important in exploiting static comparative advantage" (1984, 507). Beyond that they suggested that the strategy "has also been important in dynamically changing Korea's comparative advantage through accelerating the broadening and deepening of industrial competence" (507). They maintained that exports created a climate wherein new industries could be developed "much earlier than they could otherwise have been . . . without sacrificing economies of scale" (507). The adjustments that they described for Korea brought with them an ongoing need for successful access to foreign markets. Growth based upon such a premise may have been purchased at the expense of a certain amount of economic sovereignty.

Thus Korea and presumably other export-oriented economies, even those where government decision making has infringed upon the operations of domestic markets, will find themselves faced with forces in the world economy that will undoubtedly impact broad ranges of domestic considerations. In the case of the NIC's of Asia, the decisions that they have made may be more easily reinforced than repealed. If the growth that was generated by export strategies is to be sustained and perhaps enhanced, the governments concerned may be able to retreat from attempts at controlling their economies but will face the necessity of doing what they can to facilitate the international dealings that have become the mainstays of those economies. Ironically, the very governments characterized by Islam and Kirkpatrick as usurping the role of the "invisible hand" are now faced with the necessity of encouraging the international market linkages that have been making inroads upon their sovereignty.

## REPUBLIC OF KOREA

With respect to Korea, export activity "became an integral part of the government's efforts to promote the acquisition of technological capability more generally" (Westphal et al. 1984, 509). The exports in question were capital goods and related services. Westphal and his colleagues saw their promotion as, among other things, a way to speed up the emergence of skilled and technology-intensive industries (509). Those authors identified the leading export agents as the "chaebol"—large conglomerate business groups dating from the 1970s (510). The chaebol, together with several large Korean construction firms, have joined the ranks of the world's largest international contractors.

Among the exports of these concerns are such things as technological knowledge, technical services, embodiment activity, training services, management services and marketing services (511). In presenting such a taxonomy, Westphal and associates have focused attention upon the emerging importance of various service-oriented activities. To maintain and enhance their international interests, Korean concerns have become heavily involved in various export services. This is hardly surprising, in view of the facilitative roles of various services in advanced economies, not to mention similar roles on the international level (McKee 1988, 1991).

Although much has been written concerning the role of export-oriented manufacturing sectors in the economic growth of the jurisdictions in question, much less is available concerning export-oriented services or even services that facilitate export. When jurisdictions that have based their growth upon the export of manufactured goods begin exporting manufacturing technology as well, it seems hardly surprising that business-related services should become more important.

It seems evident that Korea has been experiencing the form of adjustment cited above. Westphal points out that "export successes in simple manufactures such as wigs, textiles and plywood were followed by rapid gains in other products like shoes, steel, ships and electronic products" (1990, 43). Beyond those endeavors he points to Korean successes in penetrating "markets for sophisticated durable goods such as automobiles and computers" (43). Success in such endeavors has come with relatively little reliance upon multinational corporations. Westphal points out that Korean successes have been nurtured by various supportive public policies.

There seems little doubt that various service activities have played roles as well. The importance of various services may become apparent through a review of Westphal's discussion of technology and how it is acquired or changed. He sees an "abundant international trade in the elements of technology, through transactions involving licenses, capital goods, direct investment, technical assistance and the like" (55). Yet he suggests that "the tacitness of much technology creates problems in communication over long distances and across social differences" (55). As "peculiarities in local resources, institutions, and local technological practices cannot be comprehended without being experienced in some way," Westphal is perceptive in suggesting that "Efforts to acquire technological capability and to tailor technology to the circumstances often coincide" (55). Modest though individual technological changes may be, their cumulative effects when they occur in sequence can be very large (55).

Westphal sees "pronounced economies of scope in the application of many of the capabilities acquired in the course of industrialization" (55). He sees transactions between domestic agents with respect to technology increasing in relative frequency and specialization with industrialization

(55). "Additional externalities can result because demonstration effects from an initial entrant's investments to master new technology may greatly reduce costs for subsequent nearby entrants" (55).

Westphal's observations seem readily applicable to various service categories geared to the support of export activities. There is little need to reemphasize the role of various transportation and communications services in this regard. The international transfer of technology cannot be accomplished without the assistance of various services geared to reduce institutional, legal and financial impediments. Technical assistance of an engineering variety may also be a significant need. In many emerging economies the types of services alluded to here are provided by service firms that have become international in their own right as they have expanded to meet the needs of their multinational corporate clients. Even in the case of Korea, where the emergence of export-oriented production was largely based upon government-encouraged domestic enterprise, external service cadres were undoubtedly necessary in the development of trading relationships.

Writing in 1990, Chungsoo Kim and Kihong Kim suggested that the newly industrialized nations of Asia have begun to see "areas of service trade where they may acquire international competitiveness" (182). According to those authors, Korea's service sector, which employed 35 percent of total employed workers in 1975, accounted for approximately one-half of the workforce in 1987 and 57 percent of gross domestic product (182). Despite that expansion, they saw Korea's service sector as "characterized by labour-intensive modes of production," thus differing fundamentally "from the capital . . . intensive service sectors of industrialized countries" (182). They attributed Korea's weak overall trade balance of services to its sectoral imbalance and pointed out that "much attention is being paid to the deregulation and internationalization of Korea's financial-service industries" (183).

## TAIWAN

Turning to Taiwan, the same authors suggested that the nation's service sector is the smallest among the newly industrialized economies of the region and "in every major service trade it has registered a chronic deficit" (184). They suggested that Taiwan "does not appear to have strong across the board international competitiveness in service trade," with its service industries facing problems similar to those being experienced in Korea (184). They did point out that Taiwan had recently dismantled regulations on the foreign exchange market, "including relaxation of restrictions of limits on foreign-currency remittance, and has begun to permit participation of foreign security firms in its market" (184). Certainly Taiwan will find itself more involved with various international services that facilitate business if export-led growth is to remain a centerpiece of its growth strategy.

## SINGAPORE AND HONG KONG

In Singapore and Hong Kong, services are even more important than they are in Korea and Taiwan. In Singapore, services have been estimated at 70 percent of GDP and 70 percent of the total workforce (184). In Hong Kong services accounted for 77.5 percent of GDP in 1987 (185). Singapore compensates for its chronic deficit in merchandise trade through a surplus in service trade (184). Both Singapore and Hong Kong have relied upon their financial sectors as growth stimuli. Hong Kong is second only to Tokyo as an international financial center in Asia, and Singapore ranks third (185). Singapore and Hong Kong have been cited as the "two most open countries in the world" (Krause 1988, S46). It is hardly surprising that they are heavily involved in international services.

Although both Hong Kong and Singapore have enjoyed some success in manufacturing exports, as have Korea and Taiwan, it may be that their futures lie more in the direction of international service pursuits. As virtual city-states, they appear never to have really shed their entrepôt roles. The specifics of Hong Kong's future are clouded by the impending changes that 1997 will bring. Presumably, beyond that date Hong Kong may become even more of a window on the world for China than it is at present. In such a capacity the significance of international services to the Hong Kong economy will most probably increase.

Electronics and oil notwithstanding, Singapore has emerged as a very significant international service center. Uncertainties concerning Hong Kong's future can only enhance that role. If Hong Kong is a window on the world for China, Singapore provides that service to a variety of countries in the region. As a longstanding and growing entrepôt, its service activities can be expected to expand apace. Certainly exports from Singapore will continue to cross the Pacific, but their importance domestically may well be eclipsed by growing service involvements.

## THE INTERNATIONAL ACCOUNTING FIRMS

As the main purpose of this book rests in explicating the importance of the large international accounting firms to changes that are occurring in the

Pacific Basin, space does not permit a detailed investigation of services in general. Of course, traditional accounting services appear to be crucial in a world economy where the importance of political boundaries appears to be shrinking. Such services are certainly among those that have facilitated the emergence of the world economy and the flow of commerce across or around the Pacific Basin.

Bavishi (1991, 424) reports that the Asia-Pacific region is dominated by four major firms: Ernst and Young International, Coopers and Lybrand, Klynveld Peat Marwick and Goerdeler, and DRT International (Deloitte Ross Tohmatsu). He points out that market opportunities exist in jurisdictions where "national accounting firms not affiliated with the leading international accounting firms are dominant" (424). Among nations where the overall unaffiliated presence is larger than the big-six concentration he lists Taiwan (424). He sees the growth of international accounting firms as closely connected to the globalization of capital markets and suggests that "As investors worldwide increasingly invest in foreign securities, more comprehensive financial statements will be required, resulting in an increased demand for the auditing and other services of international accounting firms" (428).

If anything, Bavishi has understated the international forces driving the growth and territorial expansion of the firms in question. Of course, the firms are expanding in order to continue to meet the needs of their clients, many of whom are multinational firms. As the multinational firms enter new jurisdictions by actually opening facilities or through the acquisition of subsidiary operations, the accounting firms have expanded into new territories. However, their growth has not been merely spatial. In meeting the needs of their international clients they have initiated a wide range of consulting pursuits, many of which have little direct relation to their more traditional auditing functions. Through a wide range of service offerings, both traditional and new, they have joined the ranks of various service enterprises that are facilitating international business operations while also adding strength to the various domestic economies touched by their endeavors.

Bavishi has provided a service to those interested in the progress of the international accounting firms in the newly industrialized economies under discussion. In his worldwide listings of the numbers of partners in the world's sixteen largest accounting firms, he enumerates those based in the jurisdictions under discussion. Hong Kong boasts a total of 192 partners, of whom 147 are members of the six largest firms; Singapore is home to 160 partners, including 127 from the Big Six. South Korea has the highest number of partners among the jurisdictions under discussion. Of the 250 partners resident in that nation, 139 are affiliated with the big six. Taiwan has fewer partners than the other economies, 96 in total, of whom 67 are members of the big six (Bavishi, 1991). Of course Bavishi, as mentioned earlier, identifies that nation as having a complement of unaffiliated accountants, larger in number than that of Big Six partners.

Although Price Waterhouse was not identified by Bavishi as among the leading international accounting firms in the Asia-Pacific region, its operating manual for Singapore outlines a rather extensive involvement. This manual may not be indicative of the actual operations of the other firms but it certainly suggests the scope that such operations might encompass. In Singapore, Price Waterhouse serves "a large number of major local and international organizations as well as many smaller clients, public sector entities, nonprofit organizations, and individuals" (1990c, 162). The firm provides comprehensive training to enhance the expertise of its staff and supports its operations with technical and library resources (163).

Among the range of services offered are those related to auditing, accountancy and taxation. Beyond those traditional offerings the firm provides assistance in management consultancy and corporate reconstruction and insolvency. It provides assistance with acquisitions and mergers and offers business advisory services and corporate secretarial services. "Other services include share and business valuations and stock exchange listings" (163). Among the clientele served, the firm lists "financial institutions, insurance companies and both multinational and local businesses in the industrial, commercial and service sectors" (163). With such a menu of services it seems clear that Price Waterhouse and others with like offerings are in a position to accomplish major impacts in the economy of Singapore.

In the management consulting field Price Waterhouse Management Consultants Pte Ltd., a firm that is wholly owned by the partners of the accounting firm in Singapore, offers a variety of services. "Full-time consultants with directly relevant experience in industry are able to provide a broad range of consulting skills to senior management" (164). As part of the "worldwide network of Price Waterhouse, the firm is able to supplement the skills of its own consultants. . . . Services are provided with respect to general management, and information technology, as well as finance, manufacturing, marketing and human resources and personnel recruitment" (164).

This service may well provide some stability to elements of the business community: "Our aim in a situation of potential insolvency is to be constructive, seeking to preserve businesses and create opportunities" (164).

Where liquidation or receivership cannot be avoided the firm tries to aid in maximizing realizations of creditors. Once again the firm is found in a facilitative role that may do much towards providing a stronger business climate. In its own words, "Our insolvency personnel possess a wide range of practical business skills and they believe in making a positive contribution to the economy by reconstructing and nursing back to viability businesses that are in financial difficulty" (164).

Among services offered in this area are business reviews and corporate reorganizations. Assistance is also offered with respect to judicial management, delinquent debts and receivership of debenture holders. The firm deals with receiverships and compulsory liquidations as well as creditors' voluntary liquidations and "members' voluntary winding-up" (165). Clearly, such services should serve to strengthen any economy in which they are offered.

The firm is willing to involve itself directly in the acquisition activities of its clients. Services in that regard range from aiding in the identification of businesses suitable for acquisition to assistance with the integration of such operations when acquired. Advice is available with respect to accounting, taxes and "any other matters which may arise during negotiation or completion of an acquisition" (165). Acquisition services offered by the firm are international in scope and are designed to provide advice irrespective of the positioning or type of business being considered for acquisition (165).

In the realm of business advisory services the firm is willing to coordinate a full range of business services for both large and small firms. In Singapore it assists in setting up businesses. In that regard it assists firms in acquiring operating facilities and in the recruitment of staff. The firm also provides assistance with respect to familiarizing clients with local statutory and regulatory requirements and aids in the privatization and flotation of companies. The fact that the firm maintains a Japanese Client Services department to aid investors from Japan (165) is indicative of the scope of business dealings between those two nations, not to mention how Price Waterhouse or other accounting firms may facilitate such dealings.

The corporate secretarial services offered by Price Waterhouse are especially significant in linking Singapore with the world economy. Such services include providing for the incorporation or registration of business endeavors in Singapore (165) and obtaining approval for opening a representative office. The firm can also obtain reports on credit status as well as details concerning directors, shareholders and company financial positions from records available locally (166). It can also assist by applying for employment, dependent and student passes for expatriate employees and their families (166). In addition to offering such a wide range of nontraditional accounting services, Price Waterhouse is also available to set up accounting systems or maintain accounting records. If the firm's offerings in Singapore are indicative of what the international accounting firms can do, it seems clear that such enterprises can have major impacts upon operations in the international economy while also facilitating the day-to-day activities of firms operating within domestic economies, thus strengthening those economies.

Describing its Hong Kong operations, Price Waterhouse claims to be "the largest and longest-established accounting firm in that jurisdiction," putting its current workforce (partners and staff) at approximately 1000 (1992a, 178). "The Hong Kong firm has extended its services to the Portuguese enclave of Macau and the People's Republic of China" (179). Beyond statutory audits the firm provides assistance in various areas. It offers advice on tax compliance and tax planning as well as accounting services. It also offers a range of management consulting services, "including information technology, financial management, human resources, executive recruitment, and marketing" (179). It consults on corporate finance and on matters related to mergers and acquisitions and public documents. Like its counterpart in Singapore it is able to assist in corporate reconstruction and insolvency as well as company secretarial services. Beyond the matters listed here, the firm "has also developed specialist groups that can provide advice in the following industries significant to Hong Kong: banking, insurance, retailing, shipping, property, securities and hotels." The breadth of this menu of service expertise speaks to the degree of involvement that the international accounting firms can have in domestic economies. On the foreign scene Price Waterhouse is involved heavily in expediting certain business linkages between Hong Kong and Japan. "Because of the significant level of Japanese foreign investment in Hong Kong, our Japanese practice has grown considerably in recent years to the point where it is the largest of its kind in Hong Kong" (179).

It is hardly surprising that the international accounting firms should be prospering in Singapore and Hong Kong. Those jurisdictions are virtual city-states that have a tradition of external linkages that predate their industrialization. Although both have grown in prosperity through export-oriented manufacturing, it would appear that their future prosperity may be linked more closely to various services than to an ongoing expansion of manufacturing. Neither has been involved in a major way with heavy manufacturing. Singapore has become a major center for the electronics industry, while Hong Kong has become a light-manufacturing center. The latter jurisdiction may not be able to base its future economic strength on light manufacturing, but it may continue "to export the products of such endeavors based in China" (McKee, Lin and Chen 1991). Faced with limited supplies of unskilled labor, both Singapore and Hong Kong may find their continuing prosperity linked more and more closely to various services that are in turn linked to the international economy.

The point made by the businessman quoted at the beginning of this chapter, who categorized the four NILs in question as not just super economies but rather engines pulling a whole region, seems more significant when service involvements are considered. International involvement in general and the hosting and nurturing of international services unquestionably exacts a price with respect to economic sovereignty. Yet that price may bring with it a reduction in the level of government intervention that Islam and Kirkpatrick have criticized (1986, 114).

Despite the obvious importance that trade with non-Asian partners has displayed, it seems reasonable that trade with other Asian economies can do nothing but become increasingly important in all four jurisdictions. This seems especially true of trade with China and Japan. The strengthening entrepôt functions of Hong Kong and Singapore, with an accompanying need for expanding services, has been referred to earlier. The ongoing need for expanding access to foreign markets, which appears to be the lot of both Taiwan and South Korea, speaks to expanding needs for international facilitative services.

In the case of Korea, various services are already on the books as exports, as they have become necessary reinforcements to manufacturing exports. Such things as technological knowledge, technical services, embodiment activity, training services, management services and marketing services were referred to earlier in this chapter. As has been suggested, the international transfer of technology can hardly be accomplished without the aid of various friction-reducing services. Thus it seems that, if Taiwan and Korea are to continue to enjoy success in exports, it will become increasingly necessary for them to employ the assistance of various facilitative services.

In the world economy many of the services that appear to be needed by the economies under discussion are being supplied by firms that have become international in their own right. Korea and Taiwan may find it both useful and necessary to encourage such service groups. Earlier in this chapter, Korea's service sector was "characterized by labour-intensive modes of production" as opposed to the more capital-intensive service sectors of industrialized nations (Kim and Kim 1990, 182). Taiwan was seen by the same authors as possessing the smallest service sector of the nations under discussion (184). Both Korea and Taiwan will require service expansion if they are to sustain their policy of growth through exports.

Singapore and Hong Kong have had to look to external linkages for growth, as have small economies in general. The upcoming change in status facing Hong Kong will hardly reduce that jurisdiction's international linkages. Clearly, both economies can be expected to increase their international service functions if they are to sustain and enhance their economic positions.

Among the international service groupings that appear to be important to all four economies under discussion are those offered by the international accounting firms. If the traditional accounting functions provided by those firms have not been emphasized in this chapter, it is because their importance to international business dealings appears obvious. The consulting side of their service offerings has been described, for in those pursuits the firms are having major impacts in the international economy, not to mention the economies of individual nations. In many cases, subsets of their service offerings are providing the type of expertise that was available only from manufacturers or other agencies involved in the international transfer of technology. By offering such services the firms remove the necessity, for those who need them, of seeking them from sources where conflicts of interest may abound. In short, the accounting firms, through their consulting offerings, are adding expertise to the economies in question that should assist those who use them to become more efficient, while at the same time adding strength to the economies themselves.

By offering an array of consulting services, the accounting firms may be precluding the emergence of local consulting firms. The expertise gleaned from operations in diverse jurisdictions may render the firms impervious to local competition. Such offerings may also make it unnecessary for manufacturing firms to retain staff capable of supplying such needs. They may also render it less likely that manufacturing firms will be able to export the type of capital-related services referred to by Westphal and his colleagues (1984) and enumerated earlier in this chapter. It would appear that the international accounting firms are supplying the types of services, both traditional and new, that are needed to facilitate the ongoing international dealings and linkages that the economies under discussion here will require. Other facilitative services may be needed, but the firms in question are unique in their ability to supply such a wide range of services to so many jurisdictions. This uniqueness has made them major players in the global economy, capable of major impacts within and between individual jurisdictions.

# 8

# THE FIRMS IN SELECTED EMERGING ASIAN-PACIFIC NATIONS

As international linkages have multiplied, nations at various levels of economic development have become increasingly dependent upon forces and relationships beyond their political boundaries. How this reality has impacted Asia's newly industrialized economies has been alluded to in the preceding chapter. It seems clear that various service activities are facilitating business operations in the international economy and in doing so are impacting developmental prospects in jurisdictions that are able to host activities geared to that economy.

Among the service activities in question are those introduced by the major accounting firms. In this chapter an attempt will be made to appraise the real or potential impacts of such firms upon development prospects in various emerging nations in the Pacific Basin. The jurisdictions to be considered include Indonesia, Malaysia, the Philippines and Thailand. If those nations are to succeed in improving their economic circumstances, they will undoubtedly have to increase their international involvements. Enhancing such linkages would appear to be an area in which the international accounting firms may have much to contribute.

International service firms, including the major accounting firms, position themselves in emerging nations in keeping with satisfying the needs of their customers and maintaining a competitive position with respect to their rivals. It has been recognized that "the positioning of specific business services in Third World settings depends upon the external linkages enjoyed by the economies in question rather than on what those linkages may be presumed to be in the future" (McKee and Garner 1992, 120). Thus, the extent to which the major accounting firms are operating in the emerging nations under discussion is constrained by the needs of their customers.

Writing in 1988, Thierry J. Noyelle and Ann B. Dutka were even more specific, suggesting that the international expansion of business services "is fueled by the needs of large manufacturing firms" (29). Those authors suggested that United States–based service firms often fill in expertise that is lacking in certain locations, thus playing key roles in many nations in building domestic markets (29). Accepting their logic, it has been suggested that "foreign firms may have a good deal to do with the structure and perhaps the expansion of the economies concerned" (McKee and Garner 1992, 120–21). Whether this assessment may apply to the nations under consideration remains to be seen.

With the possible exception of the Philippines, a certain amount of optimism pervades the performance and future prospects of the nations in question. *The Economist* has proclaimed Indonesia's long march from poverty to be nearly over (1993, 3), explaining that the nation has almost made the transition from agriculture to industrialism. Brian Kelly and Mark London have referred to Thailand as the next little dragon (1989). Among the strengths evident in the Malaysian economy Claudia Cragg lists "one of the highest average annual growth rates in per capita income in the world for the last two decades" (1993, 169). By contrast Cragg sees the economic story of the Philippines to be "one of fluctuations and uncertainty, far more so than anywhere else in the Asian-Pacific Rim, largely because of political factors" (202).

It may well be that optimistic assessments of the prospects of the nations in question, based upon national accounting data, may actually overstate the strength of their positions. For instance, in some nations where the availability of sophisticated business services is limited, developmental prospects may be impeded (United Nations 1987, 61). In another context it was suggested that Third World economies may exist "that do not enjoy the option of accepting or rejecting the location of various international business services" (McKee and Garner 1992, 121–122).

Certainly such services as facilitation of international business would be most likely to occur in nations such as Indonesia in settings where international linkages are most evident. "Today Indonesia is the dominant power in the six-nation ASEAN grouping, but much of its fortune is vulnerable to the rise and fall of world commodity prices" (Cragg 1993, 104). That nation is the world's largest producer of liquified natural gas (Cragg 1993, 112). Cragg sees some changes in emphasis, with the nation becoming a center for export manufacturing (111).

According to Cragg, Indonesia was enjoying a five-billion-dollar trade surplus in 1993, with real growth in GDP running at 7 percent. Presumably an export-led growth strategy should lead to the emergence of services designed to facilitate international linkages in export centers. The impact that such services, accounting included, may have on the economy in general remains to be seen. Cragg sees an immature industrial and commercial base as one of the nation's weaknesses (107) with the domestic economy dominating GDP (111). She sees the nation's economy as one of the least exposed "in terms of dependency upon global economies and specifically on the U.S. market" (112). That being the case, the emergence of international services might be expected to be slow and their impact upon the domestic economy to be modest.

Like Indonesia, Malaysia is rich in natural resources. According to Cragg, the nation enjoys one of the world's highest growth rates in per capita income (169). It is the world's largest producer of rubber, palm oil and tin (169). Cragg sees "good expansion potential with a shift to manufacturing exports . . . an increased demand for discretionary consumer purchases and country-wide development of rural markets" (169). As reported earlier (Chapter 2), "Kuala Lumpur and . . . Penang have become microelectronic production hubs for both Japanese and American manufacturers" (Schlosstein 1991, 222). Cragg identifies the electronics sector as dominating manufacturing employment with 100,000 workers and 200 companies (169). She points out that nearly one-half of the companies in question have U.S. or other foreign ownership.

Cragg feels that Malaysia is "fast joining the elite club of 'tigers'" and credits the "successful diversification of the economy away from its traditional agricultural base" for that achievement (176–177). Like the tigers, Malaysia is relying to some extent upon foreign linkages to fuel its expansion. It should be expected that services designed to facilitate international business, including those offered through the international accounting firms, would be helpful where available. There is little doubt that such services can have strong impacts in the economies of emerging nations. In the case of Malaysia the services available through accounting firms should facilitate international linkages, and they may also have a role in strengthening the domestic economy.

According to Cragg, "Malaysia, of all the Asian-Pacific Rim countries, is perhaps the easiest for most Western businesses in which to set up industrial operations" (178). The Japanese and various newly industrialized Asian economies are relocating plants there, resulting in robust growth in the manufacturing sector (180). Such adjustments generate markets for business services as facilitators of international operations. Such services, those of the accounting firms included, should reinforce expansionary forces where they appear.

According to the World Bank, the Philippines ranks near the bottom of the cohort of lower middle income countries with a per capita GNP of 730 dollars in 1990 and a growth rate of 1.3 percent for the period 1965–1990 (1992, 218). In terms of per capita GNP the nation appeared to be much better off than Indonesia, where that figure stood at 570 dollars. However, Indonesia was experiencing a growth rate of 4.5 percent.

The Philippines as a nation has been experiencing considerable political uncertainty, on a scale that has impaired its prospects of joining the ranks of Asia's newly industrialized nations. Consisting of more than 7,100 islands (Noland 1990, 79), the nation suffers from difficulties with respect to economic integration, similar in nature if not in extent to those being experienced by Indonesia. As late as 1989, agriculture accounted for nearly half of the nation's employment while accounting for only 23.1 percent of output (80). Noland points to "extreme income inequality within rural areas and between rural and urban areas" indicating that rural incomes on average are "less than half the average urban income" (80).

Growth in manufactured exports is "heavily concentrated in three industries: garments, electronic components and handicrafts" (82). According to Noland, garments and electronic industries are to a great extent export enclaves "based on highly labor intensive assembly and packaging activities, without strong linkages to the rest of the economy" (82). Whether or not services geared to the facilitation of international business can change the situation remains to be demonstrated.

Noland points out that the exports in question (garments and electronics) have been concentrated to a great extent in foreign firms operating on a consignment basis. He sees positive spinoffs such as backward linkages, entrepreneurial development and technological advances to have been minimal (82). It may be heroic to assume that services geared to assist the industries mentioned by Noland will succeed in nurturing broader growth prospects. Cragg is somewhat more optimistic concerning manufacturing prospects, pointing to a renewal of Japanese interest in the Philippines as a base for offshore manufacturing "with special interest in extraction and equipment manufacture" (207). She indicates that at least four industrial estates have emerged "in conjunction with Japanese interests" (207). Unfortunately, such developments may not form a base from which internationally geared business services may impact more general elements of the domestic economy. The benefits from such services may well be internalized by various export enclaves.

In contrast to the Philippines, Thailand appears to have far more reason for optimism with regard to its growth prospects. According to Cragg, the nation has enjoyed the highest GDP growth rate in the Asian-Pacific Rim "at an average of nearly 10 percent per annum" (299). Indeed, Thailand is increasingly grouped with the Asian Tigers as an export-led newly industrialized economy. Noland sees the nation to be in a good position to continue its successful development although more investment and a more comprehensive infrastructure will be required (77). He prescribes more investment in human capital and physical infrastructure which "would have the additional benefit of reducing urban-rural income inequality and discouraging further migration to the overcrowded Bangkok area" (79).

Cragg points out that Thailand is becoming increasingly involved in the international economy and "has started to become a major export platform for a number of companies that have relocated large-scale manufacturing facilities there" (312). She sees the immediate areas of the Asian-Pacific Rim, notably Vietnam, Laos, Myanmar and Cambodia, as very important to the Thai economy (312). Nonetheless, the United States and Japan account for a large proportion of Thai exports (22.7 and 17.2 percent, respectively) (313). In recent years the economy has shifted dramatically toward manufacturing for export. "On average, one new factory starts operation in Thailand every day, adding to the export-oriented manufacturing base" (313).

Such a manufacturing emphasis brings more expansionary pressures to bear upon Bangkok, where the needed infrastructure and foreign linkages are in place. It seems doubtful that Noland's desire for a more balanced geographical growth pattern will materialize. The services that facilitated international business will strengthen Bangkok's position as industry continues to expand in that location. The impact that such services may have within the domestic economy remains to be seen. Those offered by accounting firms will expand with the needs of their clients. If those needs coincide with the needs of domestic growth, positive externalities may well materialize.

The number and distribution of partners in major accounting firms in the jurisdictions under discussion is instructive. In his worldwide survey, Bavishi (1991) reports Indonesia as having 74 partners, Malaysia 159, the Philippines 157 and Thailand 73. Within the four nations the partners were heavily concentrated in leading metropolitan areas.

The Indonesian capital, Jakarta, boasted 65 partners or nearly 88 percent of the national total. Surabaya and Yogyakarta had four partners each, while Medan had the remaining partner. In a relatively large archipelagic nation such as Indonesia such a concentration of accounting activity in one location may not speak well for the level of development in other settings.

Certainly the activities of the firms in Jakarta can be expected to be having a "positive impact." However, the capital accounted for only 5 percent of the nation's population in 1990 (World Bank 1992, 278). If the services of the accounting firms can be presumed to be reinforcing or facilitating linkages between business firms in Indonesia and the rest of the world, those linkages would appear to be strongest in Jakarta. Whether or not such linkages will generate economic expansion in the nation as a whole remains to be seen. It must be remembered that Indonesia is one of the world's most populous nations, while Jakarta is among the world's largest metropolitan centers. Accounting services may not be present on a scale large enough to have significant developmental impacts in such an arena. Certainly it can hardly be assumed that the accounting firms are positioned to assert their influence in matters of economic integration within the domestic economy. Indeed, they can be expected to have their strongest impact in Jakarta, where they may strengthen the elements contributing to the concentration of economic activity.

Malaysia, with less than one-tenth the population of Indonesia, hosts 159 partners in major accounting firms, more than twice the number boasted by its larger neighbor. Roughly 77 percent or 122 partners are concentrated in the nation's capital, Kuala Lumpur. The remaining 37 partners are scattered among a number of state capitals and regional centers with Penang enjoying the largest concentration at 7 partners. It would appear that the firms are in a better position to impact the domestic economy through the services they offer than are their counterparts in Indonesia. At least, their positioning throughout the nation affords opportunities for strengthening economic and business endeavors and for providing national and international linkages. However, it must be said that their presence is still relatively modest in relation to the size of the nation.

The Philippines, like Indonesia, is archipelagic in nature. However, it is much smaller territorially, possessing roughly one-third the population of its larger neighbor. Bavishi notes 157 partners in the international accounting firms, all but four of whom owe their allegiance to the six largest firms. The nation's capital, Manila, hosts 141 partners or roughly 90 percent of the national total. Pasay hosts 9 partners, Celre City hosts 4 and three other centers host one partner each. Manila was listed as one of the world's largest cities as of 1990 (Todaro 1994, 250), embracing more than 14 percent of the nation's population (World Bank 1992). As was the case with Indonesia there is little evidence to suggest that accounting services are expanding significantly beyond the nation's capital. If they are in a position to impact development, it would be through facilitating certain business linkages and/or operations in Manila. At this juncture assumptions concerning the magnitude of such impacts would be nothing short of heroic.

Thailand with a population approaching 56 million in 1990 (World Bank 1992) boasted 73 partners in the major international accounting firms, all of whom are located in Bangkok (Bavishi 1991). Bangkok, with a population of 7.2 million in 1990, is listed among the world's largest cities (Todaro 1994, 250). Thailand has been rather successful in generating economic expansion through export-oriented manufacturing. Indeed, it seems to be following a developmental course resembling those adopted earlier by the nations discussed in the previous chapter. Certainly the presence of the international accounting firms in Bangkok should assist in the international linkages that export-oriented growth requires. Their impact in the domestic economy beyond Bangkok remains to be seen.

Perhaps a better understanding of the potential impact of the services offered by the major accounting firms in the nations under discussion can be gleaned by referring once again to business guides published by Price Waterhouse. That firm opened its first office in Indonesia in 1971 and operates through a correspondent firm with some 100 staff and a consulting firm with some 50 staff (Price Waterhouse 1989b, 194).

The firm sees itself as offering national and international skills in audit, accounting assistance, tax and legal advice and management consultancy (194). In the auditing vein, the firm sees its services as attractive to "large companies with multiple international activities, but also . . . small and medium-size companies pursuing a policy of growth" (195). In completing its service to individual clients it provides "in addition to an opinion on the financial statements and the various statutory reports, recommendations on improvements that the company may make in its accounting procedures and systems of internal control." By offering such assistance, Price Waterhouse or other firms have a potential for strengthening their clients. How such impacts influence general economic and business conditions in a country the size of Indonesia is conditioned by the degree to which such services become available and are used.

Beyond basic auditing services, Price Waterhouse prepares essential business documents such as annual reports and financial statements, management information analysis and manuals of procedure (195). Assistance in the accounting vein includes the preparation or checking of basic information, the preparation of payrolls, tax and employment returns, not to mention interim accounts, annual accounts and related input (195). Aids to management supplied by the firm include analyses of cash flows, financing and indebtedness and financing methods (196). Beyond such analyses the firm also does cost studies, designs cost accounting systems and develops management ratios and periodic performance statistics. It also involves itself in the implementation of computerized accounting systems and translation relating to the "fields of finance, accounting, law, taxation, electronic data processing and management" (196).

Services relating to tax and legal advice that the firm supplies seem especially important in the development of international linkages of the sort that may assist in the expansion of the Indonesian economy, not to mention private business interests. The firm sees business success as dependent "to a great extent on decisions affected by complex and changing tax, legal and financial regulations" and declares its services to be directed toward "optimizing these decisions" (196). The firm offers a wide range of services aimed at facilitating the operations of its clients concerning such matters in the Indonesian economy. Although Price Waterhouse and other accounting firms undoubtedly influence various clients and indirectly other business interests in Indonesia, as suggested earlier in this chapter, their presence may not be substantial enough to be reflected appreciably in the economy in general.

Despite such limitations it seems useful to point out services that Price Waterhouse and, presumably, rival accounting firms may be providing aimed at facilitating international business and economic relationships. Price Waterhouse offers services relating to national and international contracts. In that sphere it deals with business acquisitions and the sale of licenses, patents, trademarks and copyrights (197). It works with loan agreements and offers technical, administrative and commercial assistance (197). It assists clients in dealing with U.S. taxes. With respect to international taxes in general, it coordinates advice and assistance in different countries. It offers counsel with respect to the application of tax treaties. It does studies concerning the structure of international relations and offers assistance with respect to investing abroad. Beyond those services it also advises clients concerning intragroup transactions, not to mention personal tax matters (197).

By its own description, Price Waterhouse "provides an extensive range of consultancy services to the financial community, industrial enterprises, service companies, and central and local government" in Indonesia (197).

Such offerings run the gamut from top management consultancy to public sector services. In the management sphere the firm offers assistance in matters of strategy and business policy, financial and treasury management, production and inventory control and matters relating to sales and marketing (197). They also assist with organization and management development and management information systems (197).

In the area of information technology, Price Waterhouse offers assistance with information system designs and policies as well as with project management and systems architecture (197). The firm's service offerings also encompass communications and networking, microcomputers and the development of software. It can also assist with fourth-generation languages and data security reviews (197).

Assistance offered by the firm with respect to human resource management includes management audits, performance measurement and evaluation, remuneration and motivation and salary structures and surveys (197–198). The firm also provides assistance with executive selection and search (198).

Price Waterhouse is also equipped to provide public sector services in Indonesia. It has developed "specialist teams with particular experience in the public sector" (198). It offers services with respect to "the implementation and management of complex projects involving participants from various fields (private, public, foreign, etc.)" (198).

In offering services to the public sector, Price Waterhouse and its competitors may have a greater potential for impacting the Indonesian economy than that associated with the various private services referred to earlier. This may be especially true in cases where they provide assistance to agencies concerned with development planning. It may also be true in cases where government agencies concerned with international trade and/or foreign economic linkages are the beneficiaries. The same could be said for cases where the firms assist agencies concerned directly with the domestic economy. In short, the most immediate and perhaps the strongest impacts that the firms may have in Indonesia may be through public sector services. Whether this might be true in other jurisdictions remains to be seen.

In Malaysia, Price Waterhouse offers an array of services that parallel those offered in Indonesia to a large extent (Price Waterhouse 1990a). "The Malaysian firm of Price Waterhouse has been an integral part of the local business community for over 80 years" (187). The firm offers a comprehensive range of financial and business advisory services through seven branch offices located in the nation's main urban centers (187). The services range through auditing, taxation, management consultancy, corporate re-construction and foreign investors' support (188).

In cases where the services offered by the firm in Malaysia are similar to those provided in Indonesia, little purpose would be served by reviewing them at this juncture. However, it may be helpful to note services that may strengthen foreign linkages. Price Waterhouse maintains a team of United States tax specialists in its Kuala Lumpur office. The firm has the ability to advise and assist foreign investors to structure their investments in the most tax-efficient manner, utilizing an optimum mix of the investment and tax incentives available in Malaysia (188). There is little doubt that such services facilitate international business linkages.

Price Waterhouse has drawn upon the expertise of its various areas of practice to establish what it terms a "foreign investors support function." Under that umbrella the firm stands ready to assist with company formation and registration. It can assist in staffing at all levels and stands ready to facilitate applications for expatriate employment passes. It can also assist in applications for all regulatory approvals as well as in the establishment of trade and banking facilities. It also aids with the identification of local joint-venture partners or shareholders (189). By its own assessment the services alluded to here render foreign investors able to focus their efforts upon the operational aspects of their endeavors. It seems clear that such services, when offered by the accounting firms, may be expected to increase and/or strengthen foreign business linkages.

Price Waterhouse is also active in the Philippines, where the firm provides a wide range of professional services (Price Waterhouse 1989c). Besides accountants, the firm has systems analysts, economists, human resources specialists, project development experts, industrial engineers and investment advisors.

It seems clear that it has structured itself as a wide-ranging service supplier, equipped to facilitate business in a variety of ways. It sees itself as assisting not just its clients but also the community at large. In the latter capacity it has placed representatives in various professional, public and private sector organizations. Beyond that, its "professionals also participate in public hearings of issues involving tax, investment incentives and other business concerns" (165). Such involvements reinforce its credibility and undoubtedly advance its business interests while also impacting the local economy in ways that may be difficult to measure.

It seems quite clear that the international accounting firms, through the services they offer, have a considerable potential for impacting the econo-mies of nations that host them. However, the nature and extent of such impacts is in some ways destination specific. In cases like Indonesia and the Philippines, impacts may not result in a general strengthening of the domestic economy. Certainly the firms can be expected to strengthen the operations of their clients. They may provide training and demonstration impacts beyond the confines of their client bases. The relative importance of such impacts will be constrained by the magnitude of the firms' operations relative to the country involved and of course by the physical positioning of the firms and their activities.

If the bulk of the firms' activities in Indonesia and the Philippines are confined to Jakarta and Manila, it may be unrealistic to expect their impacts to be felt in the far reaches of the nations concerned. The impact of the firms in Thailand may be constrained by their concentration in Bangkok. Certainly in the cases cited here they should be able to strengthen the foreign linkages of their clients. They may also be able to assist new clients who are positioned to take advantage of the services offered. However, major impacts throughout the domestic economies in question cannot be assumed to follow automatically.

In the case of Malaysia, where the firms have positioned themselves in state capitals and regional centers, their potential for impacting the domestic economy may be more extensive. Impacts may also be magnified in nations where the firms have added governmental agencies to their client inventories. At this juncture it cannot be claimed that the firms have been major catalysts in the development of the nations alluded to in this chapter. However, it would appear that they have much to offer in nations relying on the international economy for their development. By facilitating international linkages they strengthen growth prospects. More general roles in the growth of domestic economies of the nations concerned may emerge more slowly.

# 9

## THE ACCOUNTING FIRMS AND DEVELOPMENT PROSPECTS AMONG PACIFIC ISLAND STATES

Nowhere has distance or perhaps more accurately remoteness been a more significant factor in the equations of development than in the small island economies that dot the Pacific Ocean. As reported in Chapter 2, contact between the islands in question and the wealthier nations of the world was rather late in coming. Hawaii, which may be regarded by some as a window on the Pacific for the United States and by others as a jumping-off point to the islands, is itself rather isolated from the mainland of North America. Honolulu is more than 2,500 miles removed from Los Angeles, and many of the islands in question are farther than that from Honolulu.

In theory, at least, advances in transportation and communications have made all parts of the globe more accessible. In practice, however, this may not mean that developmental objectives are now much more within reach. It seems clear that development for small jurisdictions is more easily accomplished when the economies in question are linked to the international economy. Indeed, sustained material improvements may be unattainable where such linkages do not occur. In spite of improvements in transportation and communications, many of the islands of the Pacific may be limited with respect to material betterment for want of appropriate external linkages.

The fact that transportation and communications technology has rendered such jurisdictions reachable hardly insures that the world will beat paths to their doors. Distance and the smallness of their markets and what they in turn can offer are all daunting obstacles.

Tisdell has made the point that distance from major economies is not the only aspect of the isolation problem facing small island economies. Also important would be "whether they are on regular shipping and airline routes and their telecommunications and other links" (1993, 2). Among those other links the present authors would include the impacts that international facilitating services are having on specific jurisdictions. There is an irony in Tisdell's reference to regular shipping and airline routes. In the case of many islands in the Pacific Ocean, it may be that improvement in the technology of transportation has made them even more isolated in some respects. For example, "Cocos Islands and Fiji are no longer on regular airline routes from Australia and New Zealand to Europe and North America respectively" (1993, 2). As Tisdell has suggested, improvements in technology have made it unnecessary for airlines to schedule stopovers, thus making former intermediate destinations more isolated.

Similar adjustments are possible with respect to shipping. Larger cargo vessels and the containerization of cargo have eliminated various ports from ship itineraries. Where this has occurred in specific jurisdictions it has resulted in the uncoupling of the ports in question from regular trade routes. What seems clear is that improvements in the technology of transportation need not necessarily impact all jurisdictions equally and that various Pacific islands may have benefitted little if at all.

Writing in 1985, Te'o Fairbairn observed that "Pacific island countries differ widely in their resource endowment and their capacity to achieve economic growth" (45). He saw the larger island countries such as Papua New Guinea (PNG) and Fiji as holding the best growth prospects. Indeed, he predicted that they could expect major changes in social and economic life as "manifested through such avenues as the attainment of higher levels of social and welfare services; greater diversification of economic activity; stronger involvement in foreign capital; accelerated urbanization; and a further decline in subsistence activity" (45).

Of course, ongoing subsistence activities and indeed the cultures associated with them have long been recognized as impediments to material improvements in various locations among the islands of the Pacific. A desire to maintain indigenous cultures and lifestyles is neither good nor bad in and of itself and must be assessed on a location-by-location basis in keeping with national and subnational goals and objectives. Destinations opting for more traditional lifestyles would have less need for international linkages. Of course, rational decisions in that regard must be distinguished from what has been occurring in very small economies where shortages of resources have combined with ongoing population pressure to insure the perpetuation of poverty.

Among the islands of the Pacific, Fairbairn has distinguished among growth economies, limited-growth economies and no-growth economies (46–54). In what he considers the lucky countries he includes Fiji, Papua New Guinea, Solomon Islands, Vanuatu and "arguably New Caledonia" (46). Collectively those countries account for 3.7 million persons or 84 percent of the total population of the Pacific islands (46). He sees each of these jurisdictions as having the potential to attain cumulative economic growth and structural diversification through the use of land, sea and tourist resources (46). Indeed, he suggests that the economies in question have already made progress through planning and "a considerable input of private foreign investment" (46). However, he attributes the positive performance of the economies in question to natural endowments. "The major factor underlying these growth performances had been successful export diversification through natural resource development" (48).

Fairbairn cites Western Samoa and Tonga as examples of economies with limited growth prospects. In such locations he sees some scope for growth through agriculture, but this he sees with future restrictions based upon limited land area and opportunities for major industrialization and tourist development (49). He sees such countries as having to contend with powerful developmental constraints. "Among the most intractable problems are the existence of rigid traditionally based land tenure systems, a low capacity to innovate, paucity of capital funds and skills, continued vulnerability to international trade instabilities and rapid population growth" (50–51).

His forecast for this middle group of countries is hardly encouraging, yet Fairbairn reserves his most pessimistic observations for what he calls no-growth economies. These he sees as the problem economies of the region: Kiribati, Tuvalu, Tokelau, Nauru and the Cook Islands (51). In such settings he sees sea-based opportunities, but the "poverty of land-based resources is severe and this combined with tiny domestic markets, geographic isolation and expanding populations, provides the ingredients for malaise and decline" (51). He points out that a few of these jurisdictions have staved off subsistence poverty through emigration and foreign aid. In the same vein, Tisdell has referred to the smallest of island economies, as MIRABE economies, "MIRABE being an acronym derived from MI-migration, R-remittances, A-aid and B-bureaucracy" (Tisdell 1993, 7; Bertram and Watters 1985 and 1986).

Generally speaking, the prognoses for economic growth in the islands in question seem less than robust. Distance and isolation coupled with resource problems, not to mention expanding populations, have combined to form formidable barriers to economic expansion. Too much reliance upon primary industries has made needed imports increasingly more expensive and difficult to attain. Import substitution suffers severe constraints because of the smallness of the economies concerned. Manufacturing for export has not emerged as a major support for ongoing growth. In such a climate it seems legitimate to ask whether or not services can fill the growth vacuum that primary and secondary pursuits have been unable to eliminate. If they can do so, it seems they will have solved the problems of foreign linkage that appear crucial in most small economies.

It has been suggested elsewhere that services that are traded internationally are very important to the growth of small economies (Amara 1993a). They can often do what primary and secondary pursuits have failed to accomplish by earning needed foreign exchange while also providing domestic employment opportunities. Evidence has been presented concerning the roles of various services in the strengthening of selected Caribbean economies (Amara 1993b). There appears to be little doubt that services have contributed substantially to both growth and development in various island nations in the Caribbean region.

Despite the smallness of those nations and the fact that the bulk of them are islands, it is difficult to use the Caribbean experience as a basis for understanding the situation facing the Pacific islands. One of the most visible international service groups in the Caribbean is the tourist industry. It seems less than appropriate to suggest that various Pacific jurisdictions can or should emulate the Caribbean nations with respect to the emphasis that they have placed upon tourism. Mass tourism seems less feasible in the Pacific islands due to the time and money that tourists would require to access them, the Hawaiian experience notwithstanding. Nonetheless, tourism does play a role in many of the economies in question. That it cannot be compared to the Caribbean experience may be a positive as well as a negative consideration. Definitive judgements on such matters are well beyond the parameters of the current discussion. Suffice it to say that international tourism, if properly planned and nurtured, has a potential for positive contributions to exchange balances in most of the ministates under discussion.

As suggested earlier, advances in transportation and communications may not have provided the automatic benefits that many may have presumed for the Pacific islands. The theoretical ability to reach such locations can only result in benefits in cases where there are reasons for reaching them, meaning reasons for linkages between the islands and the world economy or specific foreign jurisdictions. In the case of tourism, travelers may have opted for stopovers in various island jurisdictions when their flights between Australia and New Zealand and Europe or North America landed to refuel. Now if tourists come to the islands they may be more likely to regard them as primary destinations rather than bonuses or respites from other travels. Indeed, the islands may be in direct competition with Australia and New Zealand and perhaps even Hawaii for tourist dollars.

Despite seemingly tenuous external linkages, the islands must import the bulk of needed manufactured goods and of course must find ways to pay for them. Earlier discussion suggested that primary and secondary pursuits are unable to fill that need to an adequate degree. Consequently the question becomes, Are there service subsectors or activities beyond tourism that can provide foreign exchange or at least a strengthening and/or expansion of the domestic economies in question?

Writing in 1990, Ingo Walter suggested that "Countries with very small, open economies have often embraced the financial secrecy business as a way of promoting economic development" (188). Among the island economies under discussion he has identified the Cook Islands, Guam, Maldives, Nauru, Vanuatu and Tonga as tax havens (187). Various small economies in the Caribbean Basin have experienced considerable success as offshore financial centers. Whether economies in the Pacific can emulate that success remains to be seen. Any Third World nation wishing to move in the direction of offshore finance will have to convince international financial interests of the advantages it has to offer. "The onus will always be on the potential host country to convince the international financial community of its political stability, as well as the soundness of its legal system and other institutions related to conducting business" (McKee 1988, 90).

According to Walter, efforts at becoming a financial center can take two forms. "One is to become a 'functional' center where transactions are actually undertaken and value added is created in the design and delivery of financial services" (188). For the host country employment opportunities should expand. "If the country is seen by bankers as a suitable location, the need of these bankers to remain competitive will ensure a considerable influx of financial institutions" (McKee 1988, 81). Walter cites no examples among the islands under discussion.

The second form of offshore center, according to Walter, is the "booking" center, "where transactions are recorded but the value added is actually created elsewhere" (188). Walter includes Vanuatu in this category. He sees benefits as including "induced employment, fiscal contributions, and positive linkage effects to firms and industries that service the financial sector" (188). Of course, any jurisdiction that becomes an offshore financial center should experience increasing employment opportunities "in the transportation and communications infrastructure and an expanding need for legal- and business-related services" (McKee 1988, 81). Such nations may also enjoy a strengthening of the modern sector of their economies. Unfortunately, it does not appear as though developing offshore financial services will be a widespread option among the island ministates of the Pacific, although it may be of limited benefit to some.

In spite of seemingly very real limitations on the ability of the island ministates of the Pacific to improve their international linkages, not to mention their domestic economies, through the activities alluded to above, there is little doubt that such jurisdictions can benefit from an expansion of service subsectors in their economies. An overview of the beneficial role that services can assume in both domestic (national) and international economies has already been provided (Chapter 2). Various business services, for example, can strengthen domestic economies that have no involvement in dramatic service industries such as international tourism or offshore finance. One such set of services are those offered by the major international accounting firms.

"International accounting services have grown in keeping with the needs of international business or, perhaps more accurately, in keeping with the needs of the international economy" (McKee and Garner 1992, 72). The major accounting firms have shown a willingness to set up shop wherever their business clients need them. By opening branches in the Third World they are linking their host nations to the world economy and presumably strengthening those host economies domestically. The fact that these firms have emerged in the small island economies of the Pacific is encouraging, for it suggests that the firms in question feel that they can be profitable in such settings or at least that competition and the needs of their clients justify their existence.

Vinod Bavishi (1991) has compiled worldwide data concerning the number of partners that the major international accounting firms boast in specific jurisdictions. His data show that the Big Six accounting firms are represented by partners in various Pacific island economies. Papua New Guinea holds the greatest concentration at twenty, followed by Guam with twelve. The latter jurisdiction is under the control of the United States. Areas controlled by the French had ten partners (New Caledonia having six and Tahiti, four). The independent nations of Fiji and the Solomon Islands accounted for four and three partners respectively. Among the remaining jurisdictions the Northern Mariana Islands boasted two partners, and the Cook Islands and Western Samoa had one partner each.

The presence of the major accounting firms may well contribute positively to growth prospects in those settings. At the very least they are a source of procedural expertise and accounting technique that can improve procedures in vogue among domestic clients. The training of local personnel and demonstration effects from their operations can impact local businesses beyond their specific clienteles. Their international expertise may make linkages with the rest of the world more feasible. In other words, the international accounting firms are among the cadres of service firms that facilitate and nurture business enterprises both domestic and foreign.

Many manufacturing firms rely upon the accounting firms and other service-related enterprises for specialized needs. Beyond the employment opportunities that such enterprises offer, "the services themselves, through the linkage functions that they perform, add jobs to national economies and, on the international playing field to the world economy as well" (McKee and Garner 1992, 78). It seems clear that the international accounting firms are fully capable of impacting developmental processes in the island economies that house them.

Elsewhere the accounting firms have been posited to be central to the cadre of service facilitators that function in advanced economies and internationally (McKee and Garner 1992, 79). Their auditing function assists in establishing order in the economies where it is exercised. They set standards for reporting and detailing business and financial data that increase the confidence of those who must use such data. If the accounting firms have become important in the world economy through their auditing activities, that importance has been further augmented as the firms have expanded their service offerings.

Certainly the accounting firms can have positive impacts upon the economies of the island ministates that host them in the Pacific. Basic accounting services can increase the operating efficiency of such jurisdictions and various consulting services may have even stronger impacts. If the overall effect of the firms upon their island hosts is to increase the interest of international players, then they have contributed to increasing the international linkages of the islands concerned.

In another context, it was asked "why international accounting firms elect to enter particular Third World jurisdictions, particularly those that are among the smallest and poorest" (1992, 79). That question could certainly be redirected toward the Pacific island economies the firms have chosen to enter. Central to any location decisions on the part of the firms must be the potential for profit but, as is the case with any provider of business services, the firms may feel the need to expand their locations or service networks or run the risk of a declining customer base. Presumably, accounting firms will enter new settings to retain or augment their accounts. "Thus it would appear that many decisions to expand are driven by the need on the part of the firms to maintain their international competitive positions" (1992, 80).

The fact that these firms have emerged in various island jurisdictions in the Pacific suggests some potential for such locations. Their presence may improve the efficiency of host economies or at least operations in their modern sectors. A negative consequence is possible where local firms are unable to compete effectively. However, the arrival of the international firms may bring with it better international linkages and economic expansion. It may also mean that local firms are absorbed by expanding international firms with no loss of domestic employment and improved access to state-of-the art operating techniques.

As mentioned elsewhere (McKee and Garner 1992), services provided by major international accounting firms may go well beyond traditional auditing functions in some locations. Indeed, the firms have been known to provide a wide and expanding menu of consulting services to both public and private clients in numerous locations on a worldwide basis. Such services may be contracted for through the firms' offices in developed nations on occasion or may be provided by local branch offices where traffic warrants the retention of staff by the firms in question.

With the addition of nontraditional services comes a broadening of the role of the firms as facilitators of business and economic activities. They have been recognized as deepening the integration of the international economy and by doing so perhaps making it more efficient (1992, 81).

Examples of the breadth of consulting activity being undertaken by international accounting firms among the islands of the Pacific can be seen in various guidebooks produced by Price Waterhouse for use by their clients. Of course the publications in question also provide basic business, economic and legal overviews of jurisdictions where the firm is operating. Pacific island jurisdictions for which guidebooks have been produced by the firm include Papua New Guinea, Fiji and Vanuatu, three economies listed by Fairbairn as most likely to succeed.

The guidebooks form a good basis for reviewing the scope of consulting services offered by Price Waterhouse with an eye to discerning how deeply such a firm can penetrate the economies of the small island states in question. Certainly Price Waterhouse and presumably other large international accounting firms are well aware of their potential impacts in host jurisdictions. "With its worldwide network of specialists, Price Waterhouse is particularly well placed to meet the changing needs of international business. It is uniquely equipped to advise in matters relating to international operations, not only in individual countries but on a regional or global basis." This excerpt from the Price Waterhouse guide for Papua New Guinea (1990b, 152) speaks eloquently of the potential that the firms share in Third World jurisdictions.

In Papua New Guinea the Price Waterhouse practice is a part of its Australian firm. The firm has offices in Port Moresby and Lae that service a wide area with a staff of three partners, a total staff of twenty-five and "a significant group of consultants engaged on management consulting assignments" (152). The disposition of operating personnel is instructive with regard to how the firm has prepared itself to perform in the Papua New Guinea market. Each of its offices has a resident audit partner, who in turn is supported by expatriate audit personnel and local staff members with varying stages of training and qualifications. Clearly, the firm sees an advantage in training local staff. Such a training function can be expected to have a positive impact upon the local economy.

A detailed statement of purpose or philosophy of service to clients, put forward by Price Waterhouse and covering its operations in Papua New Guinea, is illustrative of how a large accounting firm may relate to a host economy, not to mention the world at large (154). Aspects of that statement bear discussion here. From its intent to react quickly to the needs of clients to its desire to contribute to the development of its profession while playing a role in the wider community, it is clear that the firm intends a positive, broad-based and expanding role in the economy of Papua New Guinea. Presumably this firm would carry these intents with it to any jurisdiction it enters. Economists could hardly be accused of being unrealistic were they to assume that other accounting firms competing on a global basis share similar purposes.

The breadth of its perceived role can be seen in its intention "to adopt a comprehensive and integrated multi-discipline approach to the provision of services, based on an understanding of the requirements of each client" and "to be part of a strong worldwide organization serving clients on an international basis" (153). If such intentions are pursued in Papua New Guinea or other Pacific island settings by the Australian branch of the firm, it may be natural to assume that linkages may be facilitated between the island economies in question and that of Australia. Thus Price Waterhouse or its competitors may be instrumental in processes of regional economic integration.

In addition to its basic accounting and auditing services, Price Waterhouse has a wide menu of offerings in Papua New Guinea. Services included cover taxation and exchange control, management consultancy, corporate reconstruction and insolvency, business advisory, corporate secretarial, government liaison and the recruitment of personnel together with training (153–154). With such an arsenal of offerings the firm has a substantial potential for impacting the economy.

With respect to taxation and exchange control the firm offers income tax planning, including international tax planning, the preparation of returns and advice on exchange control (154). If such services attract international clients and thus international financial capital, they should serve to increase the integration of Papua New Guinea into the international economy. This form of integration "may provide higher levels of needed foreign exchange, more employment opportunities in the domestic economy, and presumably economic expansion" (McKee and Garner 1992, 85). Of course, these benefits may come in exchange for a reduction in economic sovereignty as the domestic economy becomes more closely linked to the global scene. The costs and benefits of such adjustments should concern planners in Papua New Guinea and other small island economies where they may be occurring. Price Waterhouse or its rivals should also be concerned about the developmental impacts of these services.

Price Waterhouse Urwick, which is the management consulting arm of the parent firm in Australia, offers a wide variety of services. "By making use of the worldwide network of Price Waterhouse, the firm is able to supplement the skills of its own consultants with the skills of other consultants in specialized areas and industries" (Price Waterhouse 1990b, 154). The firm claims to cover the majority of business functions, including such things as general management, information technology, finance, manufacturing, marketing, and matters related to human resources (154–155). Clearly, where any international accounting firm offers such services it is involved in a fundamental way in matters that will impact not just its clients but also the economies that house those clients.

Price Waterhouse aims its business advisory services in Papua New Guinea at both small and large firms. It offers assistance to firms entering the market in the recruitment of staff and in conforming to local laws and regulatory requirements. It also aids in carrying out business reviews relating to management decision making, forecasting and marketing (155). The firm arranges for the incorporation of subsidiaries and for the registration of foreign companies. It arranges immigration clearances and work permits for expatriate personnel. It prepares localization and training programs for filing with the Department of Labor and Employment and assists firms in setting up accounting systems and in the maintenance of accounting records (155).

Another area in which international accounting firms can impact host economies involves governments and quasi-public agencies. One aspect of this can be seen in Price Waterhouse operations in Papua New Guinea. "We are able to provide positive assistance in liaising with a wide range of government departments and instrumentalities, vital in setting up and maintaining a business operation in Papua New Guinea" (155). Thus they offer their services to smooth the way for foreign firms wishing to set up operations in Papua New Guinea. Of course Price Waterhouse or other international accounting firms may also offer their menu of consulting services to governmental agencies directly. In either type of service, developmental impacts appear likely.

The Price Waterhouse Australia firm has also developed a practice in Fiji (Price Waterhouse 1989a, 84). Beginning with an office in Suva in 1957, the firm expanded to Lautoka in 1968 "to service the increasing volume of work for individuals and organizations, including their branches on the western side of Vita Leva" (84). The Fiji practice also services Tonga, Western and American Samoa, Solomon Islands, Vanuatu and New Caledonia. Although many of those smaller jurisdictions may have little to attract the major accounting firms as full-time participants in their domestic economies, Price Waterhouse operations indicate how services can expand regionally from a permanent base. Of course, the jurisdictions concerned are potential beneficiaries. In addition, such linkages where established by Price Waterhouse or its rivals may well encourage international intercourse within the region.

Price Waterhouse boasts two partners and a staff of sixty in Fiji. It indicates that thirty staffers are fully qualified while the remainder are at various stages of training (85). Of course, such training, if offered on a continuing basis to local employees, is a contribution in its own right to the strengthening of the economy. As the services offered by Price Waterhouse in Fiji are similar to a large degree to those available in Papua New Guinea, there is no need to replicate the discussion of individual services in detail. Suffice it to say that the firm, through its traditional auditing operations, not to mention its consulting activities, is certainly in a position to make positive impacts upon the economy of Fiji and of course upon other economies listed above, which it is reaching from its Fijian base of operations.

Although service linkages have been indicated between Price Waterhouse offices in Fiji and clients in Vanuatu, the firm does maintain a presence in the latter jurisdiction. "The Vanuatu practice is a part of the

Price Waterhouse Australasian Firm and operates from an office in the capital of Port Vilu. Clients over a wide area of Vanuatu are served from this office" (Price Waterhouse 1992d, 63). The firm was established in Vanuatu as early as 1972 in order "to provide professional auditing, accounting, management consulting, and financial services to both local and international clients" (63). Describing its operations in that jurisdiction, the firm indicates that through working with its other offices around the world it is able "to provide distinctive comprehensive service on an integrated basis to global clients with operations based in Vanuatu" (64). Clearly, Price Waterhouse or its rivals are well able to focus a rather wide range of expertise on clients in small economies when called upon. It seems clear that such firms have the potential for rather significant impacts in the small island economies of the Pacific. Indeed, such impacts may be higher in relative significance the smaller the jurisdictions to which they are applied.

Clearly, no one would suggest that small island economies in the Pacific or elsewhere will prosper or languish in direct proportion to their hosting of international accounting firms and all that that implies. It can be said that the firms are members of the cadre of services that facilitate international business operations in the world economy. By extending their operations to the island economies in question, they may strengthen international linkages to those economies. The firms may not be among the services that have been recognized as bringing needed foreign exchange to small economies (Amara 1993b) nor among those services that make significant direct additions to local work opportunities. Despite such shortcomings, they are strong facilitators of both domestic and international business operations and thus have a part to play in development processes.

Many of the island economies in question have been subsistence oriented and have relied for the most part on primary products for their survival. Sustainable development may be difficult to achieve on such a foundation, especially if manufactured goods are needed, for most of those will have to be imported. In some island states some economic improvement seems possible based upon externally traded services. This may certainly be the case in Papua New Guninea and Fiji. No one would suggest that export-oriented services will be able to eliminate subsistence living in those states. Many forces, some of which are noneconomic in nature, may sustain subsistence circumstances in those jurisdictions indefinitely. However, externally oriented services do hold some promise for improvement in Papua New Guinea and Fiji and perhaps in some other island states in the Pacific.

Fairbairn's assessment of development potential referred to earlier appears realistic. The services of accounting firms may not be the performance leaders among service subsectors in states where economic improvements are being realized. However, they are evidencing strong and growing facilitative roles. Such roles emerge as the firms enter jurisdictions where a demand for their services develops. Given that demand, the firms through their operations have a potential for strengthening the modern sectors of the island ministates that host them. This strengthening can come about as a by-product of the services the firms offer to their private sector clients. Of course, where their clients are public agencies, their role in the strengthening process may be more immediately visible.

# PART IV

---

## IMPLICATIONS FOR GROWTH
## AND CHANGE IN THE
## PACIFIC BASIN

---

# 10

# A SUMMARY OF ACCOUNTING SPECIFICS

In Part II of this volume, institutional arrangements impinging on accounting and business practices in various Pacific nations were delineated. Of course, those arrangements may be a two-edged sword with respect to the present strength and future potential of the economies of the nations concerned. Domestic laws and regulations, if well-designed and orchestrated, can do much to provide a stable and predictable business climate conducive to economic expansion. Such institutional arrangements, if inadequate or nonfunctional, may become barriers to economic improvement. The nature of domestic institutional frameworks is especially important if they impact international business and economic linkages.

In this chapter an overview of the institutional environments facing the nations concerned will be provided. The aim will be to suggest how well or poorly served the nations are with respect to their legal and institutional frameworks. It is hoped that such assessments will provide a better basis for understanding the impacts that major accounting firms may be expected to assert. Following the format established in this volume, the nations concerned will be presented in three groupings: the newly industrialized economies, the emerging economies and the small island economies.

## THE NEWLY INDUSTRIALIZED ECONOMIES

As was stated in Chapter 4, in the Republic of Korea all businesses except for the very small are required by the Commercial Code to maintain proper accounting books. Generally accepted accounting principles (GAAP) are formulated by the Ministry of Finance and by the Korean Securities and Exchange Commission. Such principles take the form of decrees and regulations and are binding upon all businesses, including single proprietorships. Where financial accounting standards do not contain applicable prescriptions, accounting practitioners may rely on other laws and regulations or on procedures established through general practice. As an example, Korean GAAP is impacted in many ways by principles of taxation (Coopers and Lybrand 1991, K-1).

In Korea every incorporated entity is required to appoint a statutory auditor. A corporation with assets in excess of W3 billion or with paid-in capital in excess of W500 million requires an audit by an independent licensed Korean CPA. The External Audit Law regulates the size and number of companies that a CPA may audit. In addition to audits for financial reporting purposes, the tax returns of certain companies should be reviewed and certified before being filed (Price Waterhouse 1992b, 93). Audit procedures follow English-speaking-country standards.

Korean auditors' reports resemble the U.S. standard short-form report issued prior to the 1988 revision (88). To undertake audit engagements, one must be a member of the Korean Institute of Certified Public Accountants. That organization enjoyed a membership of 2,188 registered CPAs, six foreign CPAs and 351 junior CPAs as of the end of 1989 (KPMG, San Tong and Co. 1990, 3–4). Membership in the organization requires the passing of the Korean CPA examination, which is controlled by the Korean Securities and Exchange Commission. The examination is considered difficult, with roughly 250 passing each year (Price Waterhouse 1992b, 88). In 1992 there were upward of 2,000 practicing CPAs. The Institute has promulgated rules regarding ethics and professional conduct. Such rules restrict or regulate conduct concerning commissions, advertising, beneficial interest of clients and unfair competition. Members must also participate in ongoing professional education.

In the promulgation of accounting principles, the Korean Securities and Exchange Commission is assisted by the Accounting Standards Advisory Board of the Institute and by the Bank of Korea. All companies in Korea must comply with the accounting standards. Financial reports prepared under Korean GAAP require more detailed information than is the case in the United States or Great Britain.

Accounting standards in Korea and the United States differ in various ways. In Korea the revaluation of assets is permitted in specific circumstances. Marketable securities and security investments are valued at the lower of cost or market using a weighted-average or moving-average method. Investments of affiliated companies over which parent companies have significant influences can be carried at cost even if the market is below cost value. Goodwill can be amortized over an estimated useful life of between five and ten years (Bavishi 1991, 53). Negative goodwill is entered as an addition to paid-in capital. Certain costs can be deferred and amortized over three to five years. These include such items as organizational, pre-operating, new stock issuance, debenture issuance and certain defined research and development costs.

Legal reserves of 10 percent must be set aside until 50 percent of total capital stock is reached. Price Waterhouse describes conglomerates in Korea as more akin to brother-sister relationships than of a parent-subsidiary nature (1992b, 93). Consolidated financial statements often fail to provide adequate disclosures with respect to such relationships. Such statements include only majority-owned domestic subsidiaries, with others reported generally at cost (Bavishi 1991, 54). Equity-method procedures are not required for investments in affiliates over which the parent has substantial control, except in cases where consolidated financial statements are prepared (53).

Accounting changes are handled prospectively rather than retroactively in Korea. Depreciation and bad debt expenses may be calculated using tax rules that may not reflect the basis that most closely reflects economic activity. Segment reporting by industry is not required, but reporting by product lines is followed by many firms. The allocation of income tax between periods is not permitted. Differences in classification criteria dictate that most losses be carried as operating losses. The current rate method is used in foreign currency translations, with gains or losses taken to the income statement or to shareholders' equity (Bavishi 1991, 53). Interim reports are semiannual and are not consolidated. It seems clear that a wide range of differences exist between Korean accounting and reporting standards and those of the United States.

In Taiwan enterprises can take the form of single proprietorships, partnerships, or companies. Companies with paid-in capital of NT $200 million or more can be registered by the Securities and Exchange Commission as public companies. Such firms must make public disclosures of their financial statements. Companies of the size mentioned above are generally required to offer shares to the public. In going public, companies must have audited financial statements for three years and a reconciliation of financial statement income with taxable income certified by a CPA. The CPA's comments on company internal control are also required (Soong 1992, 23).

As mentioned in Chapter 4, joint multiprofessional committees involving CPA associations have existed since 1981. The Financial Accounting Committee was given the task of establishing and updating general accounting principles. In 1985 CPAs in Taiwan set up the Accounting Research and Development Foundation, which assumed the responsibility for the Financial Accounting Committee and renamed it the Financial Accounting Standards Committee. This committee formulates generally accepted accounting principles. Such principles are supported strongly by the government and followed widely.

The National Federation of CPA Associations has issued a Code of Professional Ethics for CPAs and a series of related ethics standards. Beyond the adherence to acceptable ethical standards, all CPAs are required to pursue continuing professional education. By January of 1991, Taiwan boasted some 2,100 CPAs, of whom 43 percent were registered as public accounting practitioners. Among practitioners, 508 were self-employed while 401 were associated with some seventy-five CPA partnerships (5).

Company managements are expected to keep proper financial records and proper financial reports in the interests of both shareholders and tax authorities. Excepting computerized systems and small-scale enterprises, accounting books must be submitted to the tax authority for registration before use. Computerized systems must gain the approval of the tax authority.

All entries for transactions must be supported by proper documents. For purchasing goods and services, a unified invoice is prescribed and controlled by the tax authority. Companies with capital of NT $30 million are required to have audited financial statements. Those with bank credit reaching NT $30 million must submit the audit report and financial statements to the Credit Center of the Taipei Bankers' Association. Those with revenues of NT $100 million are required to have their income tax returns certified by a CPA.

Publicly held companies are required to submit audited semiannual and annual financial statements as well as first and third quarter financial statements (reviewed by CPAs) to the Securities and Exchange Commission. These materials must also be published in newspapers. All audits of financial statements are subject to government regulation. Income tax returns are also audited by CPAs, with the audits based upon tax regulations (12). Auditing standards are in practice similar to those in the United States. Indeed, the Taiwan standard audit report is identical to the pre-1988 standard United States report.

There are differences in GAAP between Taiwan and the United States. If prices rise by 25 percent, the revaluation of assets is permitted in Taiwan. Depreciation is taken generally on a straight-line basis, and inventory costing generally employs the average-cost method (Bavishi 1991, 88). Consolidated financial statements are required where one company controls another, with some exceptions for subsidiaries in businesses so dissimilar as to cause consolidations to appear misleading. Exceptions are also permitted for legal reorganizations, bankruptcies and cases of foreign subsidiaries domiciled where dividends cannot be remitted (Soong 1992, 54). Subsidiaries with assets or total revenues less than 10 percent of the parent company may be excluded, as may subsidiaries with shareholder equity of less than zero. Business combinations are taken care of under Company Law. Assets and liabilities of acquired companies are customarily recorded at their book value. Shareholders' equity is generally charged directly for negative goodwill (54). The method of accounting for a business combination is not disclosed (Bavishi 1991, 88).

In Taiwan, deferred income tax procedures are not required. All long-term construction contracts require the percentage-of-completion method over one year in which profit or loss can be estimated reasonably. According to Bavishi, foreign currency translations are determined by the current rate method with gains or losses from translation taken into income or deferred (1991, 88).

Generally accepted accounting principles do not cover such things as earnings per share, disclosure of business segments, future contracts, development stage enterprises and financial reporting for changing prices, all of which are covered by GAAP in the United States (Soong 1992, 18). According to Bavishi, the potential or actual dilution effects on earnings per share of senior convertible securities are not disclosed (1991, 88). Ten percent of net after-tax income must be set aside each year until the legal reserve reaches 50 percent of paid-in capital. These reserves can be used only for corporate losses (Price Waterhouse 1991a, 100). Bavishi points to the fact that footnotes to financial statements are only sometimes used (1991, 88). As such notes represent a principle means of disclosure, their lack may illustrate a major difference between Taiwan and the standards of wealthier or more developed nations.

Singapore permits enterprises in the form of incorporated companies— usually with limited liability, branches of foreign corporations or unincorporated businesses. The last category includes proprietorships, partnerships, and joint ventures. Corporations require records from which financial statements reflecting "true and fair" financial condition can be prepared. Accounting and other records must be available for the preparation of true and fair financial statements and for their audit. Public companies are expected to have adequate systems of internal control (David Tong 1993, 97). Audits of corporations must be performed by approved certified public accountants. There are no statutory audit requirements for unincorporated businesses.

Companies can be either public or private, but private companies are limited to fifty shareholders. All companies and foreign branches must file audited financial statements with the Registrar of Companies. An exception occurs in the case of exempt private companies (those with no more than twenty shareholders). Such companies, although needing audited financial statements, are not required to file them with the Registrar (97).

Accounting professionals include both practicing public accountants and nonpracticing. The latter variety includes those in government and industry as well as those employed by public accountants. As reported in Chapter 4, in 1991 there were 637 practicing public accountants (9 percent of the profession). The Singapore Accountants Act of 1987 established the Institute of Public Accountants of Singapore, which was designated as the agency to develop and disseminate accounting and auditing requirements. Under the act the Public Accountants Board was the registration and disciplinary authority (David Tong 1993). All registered public accountants must meet the requirements dictated by the Public Accountants Board Rules, which are administered by the Institute. Such requirements include the completion of the professional examination, requisite experience, pre-registration courses and demonstrated proficiency in local laws (2, 7).

The auditing standards put forward by the Institute are international standards refined to meet local needs. In fact, the standards in question are very similar to those of the United States. Auditors must report to company audit committees concerning their review of internal control structures. The auditor's report follows British practice in stating whether financial statements render a true and fair view of matters reported upon. The auditor must also report to the Minister of Finance if serious fraud or dishonesty has been perpetrated on the company. The audits must provide the trustees of the company's debenture holders with reports issued to the corporation and must also inform them of anything relevant to their duties (9). Auditors have a legal right to access all company records, and any attempt to obstruct the completion of an audit is subject to penalty.

The Institute issues statements of Accounting Standards which become mandatory. The nation has taken the standards put forward by the International Accounting Standards Committee as its own generally accepted accounting procedures. The Institute also publishes *Statements of Recommended Accounting Practice* to be used as guidance by accountants. In cases where no procedures or practices are prescribed, generally accepted accounting principles from other nations may be adopted.

There are various differences between Singapore's generally accepted accounting principles and those of the United States (70). For instance, real property can be carried at either cost or appraisal value. Any increases or appraisals are credited to capital reserves. Interest costs incurred while preparing assets for use are not capitalized as part of the cost of the asset. In cases where control is intended to be temporary, some entities are not consolidated even if control is assured. Unconsolidated subsidiaries may be carried at cost, revaluation amounts, or the lower of cost or market. Goodwill may be recognized as an asset, amortized over its useful life, or written off against shareholders' interest (72). Methods employing imputed interest are not used for receivables or payables not subject to normal trade terms (75). Separate reporting is not required for discontinued segments of a business (80). For income tax purposes, operating losses may not be carried back to earlier periods (83).

In Hong Kong, as with the other nations being discussed, business may take various forms—sole proprietorships, partnerships or corporations. Although proprietorships must register for tax purposes, they need not have their financial statements audited or made public. Specific accounting and auditing rules do not exist for partnerships, but the Partnership Ordinance requires partners to supply tax accounts and full information on all matters affecting the partnership (Byrne 1988, 28). Foreign corporations wishing to do business must register and provide required documentation to the Hong Kong Companies Registrar. Foreign public corporations must provide audited financial statements and a director's report to the Companies Registrar on an annual basis. Foreign private corporations are exempt from these requirements. Companies incorporated in Hong Kong may be organized with limited or unlimited liability. They may remain private by restricting the right of share transfer and by limiting shareholders to fifty (Coopers and Lybrand 1991, H-3).

All incorporated firms must appoint an auditor who is a CPA, with a practicing certificate issued by the Hong Kong Society of Accountants (Byrne 1988, 1, 9). Auditors report on the firm's financial statements as to whether they "present a true and fair view of the state of affairs of the company, its profit or loss and changes in financial position" (8) and whether the statements "are properly prepared in accordance with the Companies Ordinance" (8). The Hong Kong Inland Revenue Department requires the audit report and financial statements to be included with tax returns (Byrne 1988, 10).

Since 1973 the Hong Kong Society of Accountants has been the only official accounting body in Hong Kong and has had the authority to formulate accounting and auditing standards and to conduct accountancy examinations. It can also prescribe the experience necessary for gaining a practice certificate (Price Waterhouse 1992a, 9). It also puts forth various pronouncements concerning basic accounting techniques, standards and guidelines. Such offerings are based in large part upon related statements from United Kingdom accounting institutes.

Byrne sees auditing standards in Hong Kong as tending to permit more latitude for professional judgment than do United States standards, which are more codified (1988, 10). Indeed, generally accepted accounting principles in Hong Kong and the United States differ in various ways. Although historical cost is the primary basis of valuation in Hong Kong, alternative courses of action are permitted. Revaluation of tangible fixed-asset accounts and related accumulated depreciation accounts may be undertaken based on a current valuation. Fixed assets may be revalued based upon directors' estimation or valuation. According to Byrne, such variations from historical cost must be disclosed in footnotes (1988, 20).

No standard exists for disclosing industry segment information, but there is an accounting guideline that is followed by a minority of companies (81). In general, subsidiaries are included in consolidated statements. Exceptions occur when the business of the subsidiary is dissimilar to others in the consolidated entity, when the control of the subsidiary by the parent is significantly improved for the foreseeable future, or when control is expected to be temporary. No standard exists for business combination accounting, nor do criteria exist for the pooling of interest treatment. Goodwill may be carried as a permanent intangible asset except where its value is permanently impaired. Goodwill may also be charged off to a reserve account as it is acquired or to an extraordinary profit or loss. It may also be written off over a defined period of time (21). The most common practice is to carry the goodwill from a business combination as an asset to be amortized over periods estimated to benefit (79).

Imputed interest is not used for receivables or payables occurring in transactions that were not subject to the usual terms of trade or were beyond the usual course of business. As inventory methods must result in the closest practical estimate of actual cost, FIFO and average cost are widely employed and LIFO is not. No requirements exist for research or development costs. No accounting standards exist for pensions, and few enterprises have put together pension plans for their employees (Byrne 1988, 88).

## THE EMERGING ECONOMIES

As stated earlier, businesses in the Philippines may be single proprietorships, partnerships or corporations. Single proprietorships must be registered with the Bureau of Domestic Trade and are also required to hold a municipal business license. Partnership law is founded in United States law.

All taxpayers, personal or corporate, must keep books of account. Those with quarterly sales or receipts not exceeding (P) 5,000 may use simplified bookkeeping records authorized by the Secretary of Finance. The Bureau of Internal Revenue must approve the books prior to their use and computerized records are generally approved after being inspected and verified by a Bureau examiner.

Philippine corporations are governed by the Corporation Code, which is generally comparable to United States corporate law. Corporate boards must present financial reports for preceding-year operations, including audited financial statements at a regular stockholder meeting. Financial statements are required to be audited by an independent certified public accountant (SGV and Co. 1989, 26).

Public offerings of securities must be registered with the Security Exchange Commission. There are two stock exchanges in the Philippines— Manila and Makati. Both have similar listing requirements, including the filing with the exchange of the latest audited financial statements. Filings with the Security Exchange Commission are generally open to the public. Auditors are required to be independent certified public accountants.

The law governing the accounting profession in the Philippines dates from 1975 (1). To be a certified public accountant, a valid registration certificate from the Board of Accountancy is required. The Board is supervised by the Professional Regulation Commission, the organ that recognizes the Philippines Institute of Certified Public Accountants as the official CPA organization. In 1988 the Institute boasted 25,000 members, of whom an estimated 26 percent were in public practice, 18 percent in government service, 39 percent in commerce and industry, 10 percent in education and the remainder in various lines of work (6).

Auditing standards are the responsibility of the Auditing Standards and Practice Council. Once approved by the Board of Accountancy and the Professional Regulation Commission those standards become mandatory for all CPAs. Generally accepted auditing standards bear a general resemblance to those that existed in the United States prior to 1988. However, there are a sizeable number of differences between the required auditing practices of the two nations. The differences often appear in the official audit procedures promulgated, yet in practice most CPAs in the Philippines follow procedures rather similar to requirements in the United States (49–53).

In the Philippines the standard audit report is the same as the two-paragraph report used in the United States prior to 1988. Departures from the report are along lines similar to those occurring in the United States prior to 1988 (13). Accounting standards are put forward by the Accounting Standards Council of the Philippine Institute of Certified Public Accountants. The Council begins by issuing exposure drafts and, after public input, issues Statements of Financial Accounting Standards. After being approved by the Board of Accountancy and the Professional Regulation Commission, these standards become part of the rules and regulations governing CPAs.

Although there are significant differences, Philippine Statements of Financial Accounting Standards are thought to be heavily influenced by United States accounting principles (16). Consolidated financial statements are not required. The revaluation of property, plant and equipment is permitted based upon index numbers or independent appraisals. Disclosure of segmental operations is not required and thus is not the predominant practice. In many other areas no explicit domestic requirements are in place, and procedures followed resemble those in the United States.

In Indonesia company law has its foundations in the Commerce Code and the Civil Code of 1847. Modeled on Dutch laws from the colonial era, the commercial laws have not been updated in keeping with subsequent changes in Dutch law. In Indonesia sole proprietorships are the preserve of citizens. Foreign investment is under government control and generally takes the form of joint ventures with domestic participation required. At their outset generally twenty percent of the equity must be owned by locals, with the percentages of local ownership mandated to attain 51 percent within twenty years. There are exceptions and variations in the rules (Price Waterhouse 1993a, 89).

Companies may be listed on the Jakarta or Surabaya Stock Exchanges or in the over-the-counter market. The markets have similar reporting requirements. Financial reporting for public companies is still developing. The Commercial Code envisions that annual financial statements be presented at annual general company meetings, yet no overall audit requirements exist for them (Coopers and Lybrand 1992, 1-2). Publicly held corporations must have a statutory audit. Other companies must have audited accounts if their articles of incorporation call for such. They must also have audited accounts for most foreign investment entities in their contract work. Audited accounts need not accompany tax returns (Price Waterhouse 1993a, 115).

In Indonesia audits are the preserve of public accountants registered with the Indonesian Association of Accountants. The association, which is the regulatory body for accountants, boasts 11,500 members, one-half of whom are thought to be in government service. Until recently a three-year term of government service was required of graduates from accounting programs. The influence of the association does not compare to that of similar organizations in Western nations. The association publishes generally accepted auditing standards which are based in large part on United States standards.

Accounting practices are frequently preferred rather than prescribed, and alternatives that comply with general principles or practices are often used. Generally accepted accounting principles (GAAP) remain incomplete in comprehensiveness and precision. The basic concepts for Indonesian GAAP are based on an American Institute of Certified Public Accountants publication dating from 1965. Later developments in accounting principles in developed nations have also been incorporated in part into Indonesian GAAP (119). The International Accounting Standards issued by the International Accounting Standards Committee may also be used (Coopers and Lybrand 1992, I-1).

There are various ways in which Indonesian GAAP differ from those of the United States. The statement of changes in financial position may be prepared using either cash or networking capital as a basis. Only public companies are required to report earnings per share, and the details of computations are not codified. No requirements exist for segmental information on either a line-of-business or a geographical basis. Indeed, segment information is usually not reported (I-7).

As consolidation is not mandatory, consolidated financial statements are rare. Indeed, many subsidiaries are not consolidated. Either equity or cost methods may be employed in accounting for unconsolidated subsidiaries, although the former is preferred in cases where the parent has significant control of the investee.

Detailed guidance is not given for business affiliations. Goodwill from a purchase of a business is treated as of unlimited duration. The GAAP has not addressed pension costs, which are generally accounted for on a cash basis. In Indonesia imputed interest is not considered in the GAAP. Guidance for the accounting treatment of related-party transactions is generally lacking (I-7). If government authority so permits, tangible fixed assets may be revalued. The straight-line and declining-balance methods of depreciation may be employed. In the Indonesian GAAP, research costs are not addressed as such but are given the same treatment as any other intangible asset. There are no provisions for deferred taxation, and income tax expense is generally recorded as the amount of current taxes payable. After financial statements are put forward, there is no requirement for retroactive restatement in the event of subsequent discovery of accounting errors that affect prior periods.

In Malaysia business ventures can take the form of sole proprietorships or partnerships. Corporations as well as individuals may enter into partnerships. Joint ventures may be carried out by partnerships or through the corporate format. As mentioned in Chapter 5, beyond government enterprises, business is conducted primarily by private or public companies incorporated under the Companies Act of 1965.

Each company must keep accounting books and records sufficient to support the preparation of a true and fair report of its operations. Such books and records for Malaysian operations must be kept within the country. All but exempt private companies must file audited financial statements and other required information with the proper authority each year. Every company incorporated under the Companies Act must have auditors appointed by the shareholders at their annual meeting. Such auditors must be independent and are subject to government approval. They must be citizens and residents of Malaysia and must hold membership in the Malaysian Institute of Accountants.

The Institute is charged with regulating the accounting profession throughout the country. A second organization, the Malaysian Association of Certified Public Accountants, conducts accountancy exams in the country (Price Waterhouse 1994, 105–106). In practice, the two organizations cooperate in overseeing accounting and auditing practices. They also issue Malaysian Auditing Guidelines and Malaysian Accounting Standards (Price Waterhouse 1994c, 108).

The approval of international standards for Malaysian operations involves a time lag. At times the two organizations governing the accounting profession determine that separate Malaysian Accounting Standards would be more appropriate than the international pronouncement (110). By and large, generally accepted accounting principles as applied in Malaysia compare quite favorably to those in effect in the United States.

In Thailand business organizations may operate as limited liability companies, partnerships, joint ventures, or branches of foreign corporations

(Ernst and Young 1990, 19–20). Branches of foreign corporations must have approval to be established (20). Both domestic and foreign business concerns favor the limited liability company form. Public companies face severe ownership restrictions. They must have in excess of 100 shareholders, and at least 50 percent of stock must be held by small shareholders. Single entities are restricted to holdings of no more than 10 percent of the stock of a public company.

Accounting books and related records must be kept by every company at its registered office. All companies must have annual audits by independent auditors. Audited annual financial statements must accompany annual income tax returns.

Licensed auditors are governed by the Institute of Certified Accountants and Auditors of Thailand and the Board of Supervision of Auditing Practice. The Institute issues proposals for generally accepted auditing standards, which must be approved by the Board. As of 1991 thirty-one auditing standards had been promulgated. These were based largely upon United States standards (Akathaporn et al. 1993, 261). The Board, an agency of the Ministry of Commerce, is responsible for controlling the auditing profession (261). It issues practice licenses to qualified auditors and may cancel them for cause.

Thailand has been experiencing an acute shortage of qualified accountants (260). The Institute of Certified Accountants and Auditors of Thailand has the responsibility for setting accounting standards. Their standards tend to follow International Accounting Standards or United States generally accepted accounting principles. In the absence of local standards those referred to above may be used. As quoted in Chapter 5, "The general trend is to follow the International Accounting Standards" (Ernst and Young 1990, 3).

Financial statements need only include a balance sheet and income statement unless the reporting firm is listed on the Securities Exchange or is a financial institution. Such firms require statements of changes in financial positions. In many business and professional services, domestic ownership must surpass 50 percent, barring permission from the Ministry of Commerce. Such permissions are rare. A bilateral treaty exists between Thailand and the United States whereby United States corporations can have wholly owned subsidiaries or branches with few investment restrictions (13). Despite restrictions on ownership rights for foreigners, foreign nationals may manage and control companies through minority ownership. In such cases work permits and long-term visas are required.

## SELECTED ISLAND JURISDICTIONS

In Fiji businesses are found in the form of sole proprietorships, partnerships, corporations or branches of foreign companies. Joint ventures may take on the characteristics of either partnerships or corporations (Price Waterhouse 1994a, 50–51). Legislation governing corporations is patterned upon United Kingdom Companies Acts, with some modifications to accommodate local conditions. Virtually all companies are formed with liability limited to shares. Private companies may be established with from two to fifty shareholders and are not required to file annual financial statements with the Registrar of Companies.

Public companies are required to hold annual general stockholders meetings where directors present company income statements and balance sheets accompanied by a directors' report and auditor's report, if made. Public companies are required to appoint an auditor holding a certificate of public practice from the Fiji Institute of Accountants. However, shareholders at an annual meeting, if unanimous, may resolve that an auditor not be appointed.

Foreign corporations must register with the Registrar of Companies and must provide detailed information. Financial statements for the company as a whole must be filed, but a separate statement for operations in Fiji is not required. All companies in Fiji are required to keep books of account and other records in English sufficient to prepare financial statements giving a true and fair view of company operations and financial conditions. Although they are usually provided where available, audited financial statements are not required to be filed with tax authorities.

Duties of auditors include reporting to shareholders an audit opinion on financial statements and whether information required by the Companies Act is properly provided by the accounts. The Fiji Institute of Accountants, established in 1972, issues accounting standards and statements of auditing practice. Membership in the Institute is available to persons with approved overseas qualifications and to local accountants with the appropriate degree from the University of the South Pacific, who have the prerequisite practical experience. Public practice requires a certificate of practice in Fiji (64).

Where the Institute has not issued standards, accountants may follow international accounting standards or those of the United Kingdom, Australia and New Zealand (64). In general, auditing practice standards are comparable to the International Auditing Standards (5). Auditors' reports indicate that the nation's auditing standards were followed and present an assessment of the true and fair view given by the financial statements and books of account.

Several notable differences exist between the accounting standards of Fiji and those in use in the United States. At the discretion of the directors, marketable securities may be valued at market when lower than cost. The last-in-first-out inventory method is not permitted. Real property held as fixed assets may be valued upward to market by charging the increment to a revaluation reserve. Machinery and equipment may be revalued upward from cost by directors or independent appraisal. The diminishing-balance method of depreciation may be used. Investment tax credits may be taken to current income in the year received. Although the practice is becoming more common, the goodwill on the purchase of another company is not required to be written off against revenues over its life. The pooling-of-interests method of company affiliation is not used. Interperiod income tax allocation for timing differences is not required (70–72).

As is the case in Fiji, businesses in Western Samoa may operate as sole proprietorships, partnerships or in the corporate form. Company law consists of the Samoa Companies Order of 1935, which resembles legal practices in New Zealand. Companies may be either public or private. Private companies may have as many as twenty-five stockholders, who need not be citizens or residents. There are no strictures preventing another company from holding shares through a nominee shareholder, nor is the foreign purchase of shares restricted by exchange controls (Price Waterhouse 1991b, 27). There is no securities market in Western Samoa.

Branches of foreign corporations may conduct business in Western Samoa. They must keep accounting and other records and make annual filings with the Registrar similar to those required of domestic companies. The Companies Ordinance requires all companies to keep accounting and related records at each company's registered office such that a report can be filed with the Registrar of Companies annually. Such reports must contain a summary of share capital, details of indebtedness and a list of shareholders with details of shares transferred, among other things.

Public companies must file financial statements with their reports. They must also provide audited financial statements to stockholders at their annual meetings. Each must appoint an auditor at its annual meeting. Private companies are not required to appoint an auditor but may do so if they wish.

Appointed directors must be registered under the provisions of the Samoan Companies Order of 1935. The Western Samoan Society of Accountants sets qualifications for Certified Public Accountants. Auditors in Samoa follow international auditing guidelines in conducting their audits

(36). Western Samoa has adopted the accounting principles of the International Accounting Standards Committee (36).

Some accounting practices that are generally followed are specific to Samoa. The use of LIFO is not permitted. Real property may be revalued to reflect inflation. The diminishing-value method is used for depreciating plant and machinery. Depreciation on buildings is not allowable for tax purposes. Various local companies have adopted depreciation methods and rates applicable for tax purposes (38).

In Vanuatu the legal system is based upon English common law. Company law is based upon United Kingdom company law amended to cover local conditions (Price Waterhouse 1992d, 39). English and French are widely used in business. Business firms may function as single proprietorships, trusts, partnerships, joint ventures and companies (37). Three classes of companies are permitted—local, overseas and exempted. In the case of local companies, returns and other materials filed with the Registrar of Companies are available to the public. This means that a local company's beneficial owners can be divulged. An overseas company is similar to a local company but is incorporated outside of Vanuatu and must secure a permit from the Minister of Finance.

Exempted companies must carry on all business outside the country but may own them from domestic locations. Filings or official documentation from such firms are not available to the public, nor does the public enjoy access to any court proceedings involving company affairs. Exempted companies must file annual returns with the registrar, but they have no audit requirements (34).

Companies may be either public or private. Accounting and related records must be kept for all companies such that true and fair financial statements can be prepared. All local public companies must appoint auditors at their annual meetings. Private companies must appoint auditors if their sales exceed VT2 million. Companies, including exempt companies that hold licenses under the banking, trust, or insurance regulations, are also required to appoint an auditor (40).

Auditors of local companies must hold valid business licenses issued under the Business Licenses Act. No auditing standards are prescribed locally, but auditors tend to follow the International Auditing Guidelines. No professional or other group sets accounting standards. If the requirements of the Companies Act are met, in the absence of other requirements the accounting standards applied will generally be those of the country whose auditing standards are being used.

Accountants in public practice are members of the Institute of Chartered Accountants in Australia or the New Zealand Society of Accountants. Thus, the keeping of accounts and financial statements tend to follow the requirements of one or the other national body as long as the requirements of the Companies Act are met. The Australian Institute is dominant. As mentioned in Chapter 6, in the absence of other requirements the pronouncements of the International Accounting Standards Committee are generally followed (52).

In Papua New Guinea companies may be public or private. All companies must hold annual stockholders meetings at which the directors report. A statement of accounts must be provided at the meeting, and an auditor must be appointed. An exempt proprietary company need not appoint an auditor, provided that all of the shareholders agree. Company auditors must follow the dictates of the Companies Act in preparing their reports (Price Waterhouse 1990b, 53).

Branches of foreign corporations may operate in the country but must file documents of registration with the Registrar of Companies. They must have a resident registered agent who is personally responsible for their compliance with the Companies Act. An annual return must be filed with the Registrar giving current particulars and, for public companies, a copy of the annual corporate balance sheet for the entire foreign company as it was prepared to meet the laws of its country of incorporation. If the country of origin requires no such balance sheet, one must be prepared in accordance with the requirements for public companies incorporated in Papua New Guinea. Foreign corporations, which are basically the same as a proprietary company in the country, do not have to file the annual balance sheet. Branch records are only required for tax purposes. Foreign corporation branches are not required to be audited (54–58).

All firms incorporated in the nation must keep accounting and other records adequate to explain company transactions and financial position (65). The company auditor reports to shareholders whether the statements of accounts present a true and fair picture and comply with the provisions of the Companies Act.

In Papua New Guinea the Accountants Registration Board has the responsibility of registering qualified accountants, setting qualifications for registry, regulating accounting practice and investigating the activities of registered accountants. Anyone practicing accounting for a fee must be registered with the Board (66).

The Papua New Guinea Association of Accountants promotes the interest of accounting professionals. That organization has not issued guidance on auditing practices or standards. In practice, the international accounting firms in the country have used the auditing and ethical standards set by the International Auditing Guidelines. The Association has adopted seventeen accounting standards that its members are required to observe. Only two of those standards—"Profit and loss statement" and "Materiality in financial statements"—were prepared and issued locally. The remaining fifteen are international standards considered relevant to local conditions. These represent roughly half of the international standards currently in force (67).

Unlike United States procedure, all income and expense, whether relating to prior periods or not, accounting errors or the like, are included in net profit of the period. If marketable securities value is below the current market price, adjustments are made at the discretion of the directors. The last-in-first-out inventory method is prohibited. The direct-costing method may be used for inventory. If real property is not held for resale, an increase in value above cost may be booked in the asset account with the offset to a revaluation reserve. In addition to cost machinery and equipment may include a directors' or independently determined revaluation amount. Investment tax credits provided as investment incentives are charged to income in the period received (71, 72). Pooling is not a recognized method for affiliating companies. Unconsolidated affiliated company investment may be carried at either the equity or the cost method.

## SOME CONCLUDING OBSERVATIONS

It is clear that accounting practices are both defined and governed by combinations of public and private prescriptive agencies within the various jurisdictions discussed in this chapter. All of the nations in question have laws in place concerning the specifics of how business firms are permitted to operate and what financial documents those firms must provide to insure that they are following the rules. Some of the laws are modeled after those of various developed nations. For instance, in jurisdictions that are or have been under the control of Great Britain, the legal frameworks bear some resemblance to the laws of that nation. Dutch influence can be seen in Indonesia, while that of the United States can be seen in the Philippines. Despite such resemblances, in most cases the jurisdictions concerned have established laws and operating procedures that reflect the specific needs of their domestic economies and business operations within them.

Generally speaking, all of the nations referred to in this chapter have organizations or agencies that prescribe what one must accomplish to be able to practice as a professional accountant. Although certain specifics differ from jurisdiction to jurisdiction, it is clear that entry into the profession is carefully monitored. This provides certain assurances to business firms that may require the services of auditors or accountants. In some of the larger or more developed nations under consideration, the ranks of the accounting profession are quite extensive. Thailand appears to be the only jurisdiction with a definite shortage of accountants.

Of course, the number of practitioners alone may not be a good surrogate for the impact of the profession within a nation. To derive a fuller picture, one must examine the size of the profession against a backdrop of what the laws of the land expect from it. There is also the matter of the location of practicing accountants within specific nations and their ability to supply their expertise throughout their territory. As the present volume is more concerned with the role and impact of the major international accounting firms, space has not permitted much detail concerning the spacial positioning of domestic accounting operations.

With the emergence of the global economy, international linkages and operations have become crucial elements in the development potential and material strength of the jurisdictions under consideration. Indeed, the four newly industrialized nations discussed here elected export-oriented development strategies. It appears as though the cohort of emerging nations are following suit. It seems as though the island jurisdictions discussed will have little choice but to seek ongoing and perhaps stronger international linkages if they hope to improve their circumstances.

Although domestic laws and procedures are important to the generation of a strong business climate, how those laws and procedures impact international linkages and business operations is also important. The compatibility of domestic laws and procedures with the operation of international business interests will encourage or retard such operations. In the jurisdictions under discussion, provision has been made for the operation of foreign subsidiaries, in some cases with local participation requirements. In general, accounting practices with respect to international operations seem somewhat less defined than are domestic procedures.

In all cases it seems clear that foreign business interests are faced with numerous domestic procedures and requirements that may be quite different from those of the nations in which they are incorporated. Those business interests must conform to those procedures if they wish to operate in the jurisdictions in question. It appears that the rules and institutional arrangements that are the subject of this chapter provide frameworks for operating stability in the domestic economies concerned. Such frameworks may be reassuring to foreign interests concerned with establishing business deal-

# 11

---

# ACCOUNTING SERVICES, GROWTH, AND CHANGE IN THE PACIFIC BASIN

---

This volume has attempted to assess the role played by major international accounting firms in various nations in the Pacific Basin. In exploring how change has been occurring in those jurisdictions, it has pointed out where possible the various services that the firms have been providing in an attempt to arrive at an understanding of how those services are strengthening domestic economies and improving international linkages.

The current chapter will summarize the economic situations facing the various economies that have been discussed. It will also review the major specifics of the contributions that the firms are making in the three sub-groupings of nations that have been discussed. First of all, the situation among the newly industrialized nations of the region will be summarized. Following that, similar treatments will be afforded the emerging nations that have been considered and the island economies of the Pacific. The chapter will conclude with some general observations.

## THE NEWLY INDUSTRIALIZED ECONOMIES

Among the newly industrialized economies known as the "Asian Tigers," the basis for growth rests with their decision to promote export-oriented manufacturing. Their outward-looking growth strategy was pursued through "widespread government intervention and control" with the possible exception of the Hong Kong case (Islam and Kirkpatrick 1986, 114). Of course, a successful export strategy presumed the emergence of international linkages, linkages that have brought the economies in question into a more significant participation in the global economy. Any real under-standing of this participation requires a recognition of the role that services have played. Among service categories with the potential for significant contributions to the ongoing expansion of the economies in question are those offered by the international accounting firms.

In the case of the newly industrialized economies in question, their decisions with respect to exports may be more easily reinforced than repealed. Indeed, the governments concerned may be well advised to do their best to facilitate the international dealings that have become central to their economies.

As has been reported (Chapter 7) in the case of Korea, export activity with respect to capital goods and related services "became an integral part of the government's efforts to promote the acquisition of technological capability more generally" (Westphal et al. 1984, 509). Westphal and his colleagues focused upon the emerging importance of various services, finding that Korean concerns have become heavily involved in various export services. Such an involvement seems hardly surprising, considering the facilitative roles that certain services have assumed both in advanced economies and internationally (McKee 1988, 1991).

When nations where growth has been based upon the export of manu-factured goods began exporting the technology of manufacturing, it seems less than surprising that business-related services should become more important. Korea appears to be experiencing such adjustments, in the course of which Westphal sees an "abundant international trade in the elements of technology through transactions involving licenses, capital goods, direct investment, technical assistance and the like" (1990, 55).

As suggested earlier (Chapter 7), "The international transfer of technol-ogy cannot be accomplished without the assistance of various services geared to reduce institutional, legal and financial impediments." Additional needs may arise with respect to technical assistance of an engineering variety. In many jurisdictions the types of services referred to are supplied by service firms that have become international in scope themselves.

It has been suggested that the newly industrialized nations of Asia have begun to see "areas of service trade where they may acquire international competitiveness" (Kim and Kim 1990, 182). Despite growth in services, Korea was perceived to have a service sector "characterized by labour intensive modes of production," thus being fundamentally different "from the capital . . . intensive service sectors of industrialized countries" (182). Taiwan's service sector was perceived to be the smallest among the newly industrialized economies of the region, failing to have "strong across-the-board international competitiveness in service trade" (184).

In Singapore and Hong Kong, services are more significant. Both economies have relied upon their financial sectors as growth stimuli. Although both have enjoyed a certain level of success with manufacturing exports, their futures may be more closely related to international service pursuits. Both are virtual city-states with traditional roles as entrepôts, and external linkages predating industrialization in both jurisdictions. Although both Singapore and Hong Kong have grown in prosperity through export-oriented manufacturing, it seems as though their future prosperity may depend more upon services.

Among the services that may have a role in that future prosperity are those offered by the international accounting firms. Bavishi saw the growth of those firms as closely connected to the globalization of capital markets (1991, 424). As emphasized more than once in this volume, the firms are expanding in keeping with the needs of their clients, many of whom are multinational firms. The growth of the accounting firms has not been merely geographical. The needs of their clients have prompted them to introduce a wide range of consulting services, many of which have little relation to their more traditional functions. With this wider range of offered services, the firms joined the ranks of various service enterprises that are facilitating the operations of multinational enterprise while simultaneously strengthening domestic economies hosting their operations.

The range of services offered by Price Waterhouse in Singapore is indicative of what the accounting firms can do. In Singapore the firm serves "a large number of major local and international organizations as well as many smaller clients, public sector entities, nonprofit organizations and individuals" (1990c, 162). In addition to its traditional offerings, the firm provides management consultancy services and assistance with corporate reconstruction and insolvency. It helps with acquisitions and mergers and provides business advisory services and corporate secretarial services. Among its clientele, the firm lists "financial institutions, insurance companies and both multinational and local businesses in the industrial, commercial and service sectors" (163). If what Price Waterhouse offers in Singapore is typical of what the international accounting firms can do, it seems clear that they can impart major impacts in jurisdictions that host them.

In Singapore, Price Waterhouse offers a wide range of services through a wholly owned consulting subsidiary. "Full-time consultants with directly relevant experience in industry are able to provide a broad range of consulting skills to senior management" (164). Assistance is provided with respect to general management and information technology together with finance, manufacturing, marketing and human resources as well as personnel recruitment" (164).

The firm appears to be asserting itself in facilitative roles that may make major contributions to a stronger business climate. In the area of corporate reconstruction and insolvency, the firm assists banks in assessing the future prospects and/or viability of customers with financial problems, thus adding to the stability of the business community (164). According to Price Waterhouse, "Our insolvency personnel . . . believe in making a positive contribution to the economy by reconstructing and nursing back to viability businesses that are in financial difficulty" (164). Such services should certainly strengthen economies in which they are available.

Price Waterhouse is also willing to involve itself directly in the acquisition activities of its clients. Such services include the identification of suitable acquisition targets as well as help in integrating post-acquisition operations. The acquisition services offered by the firm are international and available regardless of the type of business being considered for acquisition (165).

Judging from its operations in Singapore, the firm is very involved in performing international linkage functions. Clearly such functions may be offered in other locations and by other accounting firms. In Singapore, Price Waterhouse maintains a Japanese Client Services department to assist investors from Japan (165). This of course is indicative of the scope of dealings between the two nations, as well as of how an accounting firm might facilitate such operations. Through its corporate secretarial services, Price Waterhouse is linking Singapore to the global economy. It provides for the incorporation or registration of business endeavors and obtains approval for the opening of representative offices (165). It can also obtain needed information such as credit reports and details concerning directors, shareholders and company financial positions from records that are available locally (166).

In Hong Kong, Price Waterhouse has extended its services to Macao as well as to the People's Republic of China (1992a, 179). The firm has established specialist groups designed to give advice in certain industries significant to Hong Kong. Notable among such industries are banking, insurance, retailing, shipping, property, security, and hotels. Certainly such a wide range of specialized service offerings demonstrates the depth of involvement that international accounting firms can have in the economies hosting them.

The point made when the four newly industrialized economies under discussion here were categorized as engines pulling a whole region (Chapter 7) seems even more pertinent in the light of their service involvements. Although international involvements in general, not to mention the hosting and nurturing of international services, may carry a price measured in terms of reductions in economic sovereignty, they have certainly assisted in the strengthening of the economies concerned. The growing entrepôt roles of Hong Kong and Singapore, accompanied by expanding service needs, have already been mentioned. The continuing need for increasing access to foreign markets on the part of both Taiwan and South Korea will undoubtedly strengthen the demand in those jurisdictions for international facilitative services.

Services offered by the international accounting firms are among international service groups that seem important to all four economies under discussion here. Beyond their traditional accounting services, the firms are impacting the international economy and the economies of various nations through the widening range of consulting services they offer. Through their consulting offerings, the firms are adding expertise to the jurisdictions in question, which through assisting the users should further strengthen the host economies themselves.

It seems as though the accounting firms are supplying services that facilitate ongoing international dealings and/or linkages needed by the newly industrialized economies under discussion. Although other facilitative services may be needed, the accounting firms have a unique ability to supply a wide range of services to many jurisdictions. They have become major contributors to the global economy, capable of significant impacts both within and between individual jurisdictions.

## THE EMERGING ECONOMIES

With the expansion of international linkages, nations at all levels of economic development are becoming ever more dependent upon forces and events beyond their boundaries. It seems quite evident that various service activities, through facilitating roles in the international economy, are impacting the development potential of various nations in which they are available. For instance, the emerging nations of the Pacific Basin highlighted in Chapter 8 will have to pursue their development goals as components of the global economy and in doing so will be impacted by the presence or absence of various services that facilitate international transactions and linkages.

As has been emphasized in this volume, international service firms, including those in accounting, locate in emerging nations in accordance with the needs of their customers and of course their own need to maintain a competitive position with respect to their rivals. At this juncture it seems worth repeating that "the positioning of specific business services in Third World settings depends upon external linkages enjoyed by the economies in question rather than on what those linkages may be presumed to be in the future" (McKee and Garner 1992, 120). Thus it can be presumed that the degree of involvement of the major accounting firms in Indonesia, Malaysia, the Philippines and Thailand is constrained by the needs of their customers.

Some have suggested that the international expansion of business services is really determined by the needs of large manufacturing firms and that United States-based service firms often provide expertise that certain locations lack, thus assuming key roles in domestic market expansion in many nations (Noyelle and Dutka 1988, 29). Thus, foreign firms may influence both the structure and perhaps the expansion of the jurisdictions concerned (McKee and Garner 1992, 120–121).

Save for the case of the Philippines, a degree of optimism prevails with respect to the performance and expansion potential of the nations in question (Chapter 8). However, to the extent that the optimism is based upon national accounting data, it may overstate the strength of their positions. For example, in nations where the availability of business services is limited, development prospects may be impeded (United Nations 1987, 61). It must be remembered that some Third World economies may "not enjoy the option of accepting or rejecting the location of various international business services" (McKee and Garner 1992, 121–122).

In nations such as Indonesia, the services that facilitate international business are most likely to position themselves where international linkages are most evident. Export-led growth strategies should be expected to generate such service groupings in export centers. In Indonesia, domestic concerns rather than exports dominate GDP, indicating an immature industrial and commercial base (Cragg 1993, 107–111). In such a setting the expansion of international services may be slow and their impact upon the domestic economy modest.

In the case of Malaysia, Cragg saw "good expansion potential with a shift to manufacturing exports . . . an increased demand for discretionary consumer purchases and country-wide development of rural markets" (169). She sees Malaysia as "fast joining the elite club of 'tigers'" and credits the successful diversification of the economy away from agriculture (176–177).

Malaysia is relying upon foreign linkages to fuel its expansion and thus can be expected to benefit from any services that strengthen such linkages. The Japanese and various newly industrialized Asian economies are relocating plants in Malaysia and in doing so are creating markets for business services.

The Philippines, with its many islands, suffers from difficulties in the area of economic integration, as does Indonesia. Manufacturing for export is heavily concentrated in garments, electronic components and handicrafts (Noland 1990, 82). Of those industries, all but handicrafts are based upon assembly and packaging activities with less than strong linkages to the rest of the economy (82). A more optimistic view of manufacturing prospects points to Japanese interests (Cragg 1994, 207). However, as mentioned in Chapter 8, this may not form a foundation from which internationally focused business services may impact the domestic economy.

In Thailand, the prognosis for growth appears to be more optimistic. That nation is often grouped with the Asian Tigers as an export-led, newly industrialized economy. However, the increasing manufacturing emphasis has focused more pressure upon the Bangkok area. As industrial expansion continues in that location, the services that facilitate international business will strengthen the position of the city. How they may impact the rest of the nation remains to be seen. Of course, the offerings of the accounting firms will expand in keeping with the needs of their clients. Positive externalities may be realized if client needs coincide with the needs of domestic growth.

The spreading effects from services offered by accounting firms may not translate into domestic growth in the archipelagic nations of Indonesia and the Philippines. As was the case in Thailand, the accounting firms in Indonesia are most evident in the nation's largest city. If the services of the firms are assisting with the linking of business interests in Indonesia to the rest of the world, those linkages are most evident in Jakarta. However, accounting services may not be available on a scale sufficient to have significant and identifiable developmental impacts upon the nation as a whole. Their strongest impact can be presumed to target Jakarta, where they may actually reinforce the elements contributing to economic concentration.

The Philippines is much smaller territorially and possesses a population one-third as large as that of Indonesia. Roughly 90 percent of the partners in the international accounting firms are located in Manila (Bavishi 1991). As is the case in Indonesia, there is little evidence to suggest that accounting services are expanding significantly beyond the nation's capital. Any impact that they can be presumed to have upon development appears to be centered upon facilitating various business operations in Manila.

Malaysia, with a population less than one-tenth the size of that of Indonesia, boasts more than twice as many partners in the major accounting firms as does its larger neighbor. More than three-quarters of those partners are based in Kuala Lumpur. The remainder are scattered among a number of state capitals and regional centers. As stated in Chapter 8, it appears as though the firms "are in a better position to impact the domestic economy than are their counterparts in Indonesia." Their positioning provides opportunities for assisting economic and business endeavors while also generating both domestic and international linkages.

Earlier, in Chapter 8, business guides published by Price Waterhouse were used as a source of information concerning the extent of services that can be offered by a major accounting firm in the jurisdictions under discussion. In Indonesia the firm sees itself as offering national and international skills in audit, accounting assistance, tax and legal advice and management consultancy (1989b, 194). With respect to auditing, the firm sees its services as attractive to both large firms with multiple international operations and small and medium-size firms interested in expansion (195).

How such services impact general economic and business conditions in a country as large as Indonesia depends upon the level of service availability and use. In such a large country the service presence may not be large enough to have appreciable impacts upon the economy. Nonetheless, the accounting firms should certainly be able to strengthen the operations of their clients. They may generate training and demonstration effects beyond the realm of their client base. However, the relative importance of such impacts will be influenced by the extent of the firms' operations relative to the size of the country involved, not to mention the physical positioning of the firms and their operations.

In the present context it might be over-optimistic to cite the international accounting firms as major catalysts in the economic expansion of the nations alluded to in this section. However, it seems clear that the firms have much to offer in nations relying upon foreign linkages for their development. More general impacts upon the growth of the economies of the nations in question may be slower to materialize.

Although the impacts of the firms may be limited by local circumstances, they do have a wide range of services to offer clients. In Indonesia, Price Waterhouse offers various aids to management, including the analysis of cash flows, financing and indebtedness and financing methods (196). In addition, the firm does cost studies, designs cost accounting systems and develops management ratios and periodic performance data. It is involved in the implementation of computerized accounting systems and translation relating to the "fields of finance, accounting, law, taxation, electronic data processing and management" (196).

In Indonesia, as indicated in Chapter 8, Price Waterhouse "provides an extensive range of consultancy services to the financial community, industrial enterprises, service companies, and central and local government" (197). The offerings of the firm range from top management consultancy to public sector services. They include services with respect to "the implementation and management of complex projects involving participants from various fields (private, public, foreign, etc.)" (198).

When the firms offer their services to the public sector they may increase their chances of impacting the economies hosting them. This is most probable when services are provided to agencies concerned with developmental issues or to those dealing with international trade or foreign economic linkages. Of course, the services of the firms may impact their host economies through any services offered to agencies concerned with those economies.

In Malaysia, Price Waterhouse maintains a team of specialists concerned with tax matters relating to the United States in its Kuala Lumpur office. The firm helps foreign investors to structure their affairs in a tax-efficient manner (Price Waterhouse 1990a, 188). Certainly an accounting firm providing such a service can be expected to facilitate and encourage international business linkages. Price Waterhouse has drawn upon its experience to establish a foreign-investors support function. Among services provided under that umbrella are assistance in the attainment of expatriate employment passes and also in identifying local joint-venture partners or shareholders (189). The services of the firm are designed to permit foreign investors to focus their efforts toward the operational aspects of their endeavors. Certainly such services should strengthen and expand foreign business linkages.

In the Philippines the firm has established itself as a wide-ranging service provider (Price Waterhouse 1989c). It sees itself as assisting the community at large as well as its clients. Indeed, it has represented itself in various professional, public and private sector organizations, and in addition its "professionals also participate in public hearings of issues involving investment incentives and other business concerns" (165). As suggested in Chapter 8, "Such involvements reinforce their credibility and undoubtedly advance their business interests while at the same time impacting the local economy in ways which may be difficult to measure."

In the Philippines, as in Indonesia, the impact of the accounting firms may not result in a general strengthening of the domestic economy because of the archipelagic nature of the country. Impacts in the capital (Manila) may not be strongly felt elsewhere, particularly in other islands and/or more remote settlements. Indonesia, as suggested, is facing similar constraints. Thailand too may find the impact of the firms constrained by their concentration in Bangkok. Certainly the firms in the three nations alluded to in this paragraph should be able to strengthen the foreign linkages of their clients and to assist new clients who are in a position to enlist their services. In the case of Malaysia, where the firms have penetrated state capitals and regional centers, they may be better able to impact the national economy more extensively.

## THE SMALL ISLAND ECONOMIES

As suggested in Chapter 9, advances in transportation and communications have made all parts of the globe more accessible. If such accessibility means better linkages to the international economy, on the surface at least, the improvements in question might be thought to have benefitted the small island states of the Pacific. Unfortunately it appears as though improvements in transportation have left many of the islands in question even more isolated in some ways. For example, improvements in the technology of air travel have eliminated the necessity for stopovers (Tisdell 1993, 2). Similarly, larger cargo vessels, coupled with containerization of cargo, have eliminated various ports from ship itineraries. Faced with such changes, many small island economies in the Pacific are finding it even more difficult to maintain links with the international economy.

Those islands where more traditional lifestyles prevail have less need for international linkages. If island societies opt for maintaining such lifestyles, they are also opting for lesser levels of modernization and development. Cases where such a direction has been elected should be distinguished from what has been occurring in some island economies where resource shortages and population increases appear to be insuring the perpetuation of poverty.

Among the poorest of island jurisdictions are those that have been characterized by Fairbairn as no-growth economies—Kiribati, Tuvalu, Tokelau, Nauru and the Cook Islands (1985, 51). In those economies, the "poverty of land-based resources is severe and this combined with tiny domestic markets, geographic isolation and expanding populations, provides the ingredients for malaise and decline" (56). As suggested earlier in this volume, too much reliance upon primary industries has made imports increasingly more expensive and difficult to attain. Manufacturing activity has been hampered by the smallness of local markets and has not emerged as a support for ongoing growth through exports.

If primary and secondary pursuits appear to be unlikely vehicles for development in the poorer island jurisdictions of the Pacific, it seems reasonable to ask whether or not services can play a more positive role. In some smaller economies, offshore financial centers for example, certain services have provided both positive foreign linkages and domestic employment opportunities. Services that are traded internationally are very significant in the growth of small economies (Amara 1993a). Beyond domestic employment opportunities, Amara suggests that services earn needed foreign exchange. Her work has left little doubt concerning the substantial contribution of services to both growth and development in various Caribbean nations. Whether her findings vis-à-vis the Caribbean can translate into options for the Pacific islands remains to be seen.

As suggested in Chapter 9, advances in transportation and communications have not provided the automatic benefits that many may have presumed for the Pacific islands. The capability of reaching such locations can result in benefits only where there are viable business reasons for linking the islands with the world economy or specific locations abroad. In spite of rather tenuous foreign linkages, the islands must import and pay for the bulk of needed manufactured goods. The question remains as to whether certain services can contribute to balancing trade equations and perhaps strengthening or expanding the domestic economies in question.

It seems to be rather unlikely that many of the islands in question will emerge as major offshore financial centers. To do so, potential hosts would have to convince the international financial community of their stability and their ability to conduct such affairs. Even jurisdictions both willing and able to supply such services will be faced with the problem of whether or not they are needed. In a world already cluttered with would-be financial centers, entry into the ranks of successful centers may be difficult.

Despite limited potential in the international financial services arena, it still appears as though the islands in question may be able to benefit from the expansion of service subsectors in their economies. There are various business services, capable of strengthening domestic economies, which are not as visible as dramatic international service industries such as tourism or offshore finance.

One set of business-related services fitting that description are those that are being provided by the major international accounting firms. The firms themselves have displayed a willingness to offer their services wherever their clients need them. By establishing branches in emerging nations, they are linking those jurisdictions to the global economy and simultaneously strengthening the domestic economies of the nations concerned. As mentioned in Chapter 9, the fact that the firms have emerged in the Pacific islands is encouraging, as it suggests that they see profit opportunities or at the very least a client base warranting their presence.

Certainly the activities of the firms should strengthen the economies of the island nations hosting them. The firms are a source of expertise that can improve various procedures in vogue among domestic clients. Through the training of local personnel and demonstration effects from their operations, their impacts can be felt well beyond their client base. As was suggested earlier, their international expertise may make linkages with the rest of the world more feasible. They can certainly be numbered among services that facilitate and nurture both domestic and international business linkages. It seems clear that the international accounting firms are quite capable of impacting developmental processes in the island economies in which they operate.

It has been suggested that the accounting firms are central to the group of service facilitators that function in advanced economies and internationally (McKee and Garner 1992, 79). Through their auditing activities, they help establish order in their host jurisdictions. By setting standards for reporting business and financial data, they increase the confidence of those using the data. As their activities have expanded beyond auditing, their importance has increased in the world economy. Certainly the firms should be expected to have positive impacts upon the economies of the Pacific island jurisdictions that host them. Their basic accounting services increase the operating efficiency of such jurisdictions, and their expanding menus of consulting services may have even stronger impacts. If their activities in the Pacific islands heighten the interest of international players, they are improving the international linkages of the islands in question.

The statement by Price Waterhouse quoted in Chapter 6 illustrates that firm's awareness of its potential impact in host jurisdictions: "With its worldwide network of specialists, Price Waterhouse is particularly well placed to meet the changing needs of international business. It is uniquely equipped to advise in matters relating to international operations, not only in individual countries but on a regional or global basis" (1990b, 152). Although the Price Waterhouse statement speaks to the firm's own capabilities, it seems clear that other major accounting firms share the potential for such impacts.

In the case of Price Waterhouse, its intent seems clear from the statement regarding its operations in Papua New Guinea. It intends to play a positive, broad-based and expanding role in the economy through reacting quickly to client needs, assisting in the development of the profession and playing a role in the wider community (154). Other accounting firms competing on a global basis must be assumed to have similar intents in jurisdictions that host them. If Price Waterhouse and/or its competitors operate in that way in various Pacific islands, they can be presumed to be encouraging international linkages.

As mentioned earlier, Price Waterhouse offers a wide menu of services beyond basic accounting and auditing. In Papua New Guinea such services include exchange control, management consultancy, corporate reconstruction and insolvency, business advisory, corporate secretarial, government liaison and recruitment of personnel, together with training (153–154). Such services, whether offered by the firm in question or its rivals, should serve to strengthen the economies involved. Where international interests are involved, the firms through their actions certainly assist in integrating jurisdictions that host them into the global economy.

The international accounting firms can impact host economies through working with governments and quasi-public agencies. As Price Waterhouse has indicated with respect to Papua New Guinea, "We are able to provide positive assistance in liaising with a wide range of government departments and instrumentalities, vital in setting up and maintaining a business operation" (155). Price Waterhouse or other firms may also offer their services to governmental agencies directly.

It seems evident that Price Waterhouse and its rivals are able to offer a wide range of expertise to public and private clients. Certainly such firms have the potential for major impacts in the small islands of the Pacific. As suggested in Chapter 9, the impacts in question may be higher in significance the smaller the jurisdictions to which they are applied. This hardly means that the small island economies of the Pacific will prosper or stagnate in direct proportion to their hosting of international accounting firms. However, the firms in question are members of the group of services that facilitate international business operations in the global economy. Any operations undertaken by them in the small island economies of the Pacific should strengthen international linkages to those economies. As strong facilitators of domestic and international business operations, they should be expected to contribute to development processes.

## SOME CONCLUDING OBSERVATIONS

Although it seems clear that various business services, including those offered by the major accounting firms, can influence economic events in nations of all sizes and degrees of development, it is also clear that the nature and strength of such influences can vary widely from jurisdiction to jurisdiction. Such variations are certainly apparent between the individual economies and groups of economies that have been alluded to in the present volume.

Certainly nations that cast their lots with export industries will have definite and increasing needs with respect to services that facilitate international business operations. All of the newly industrialized economies that have been discussed in the present volume fall within this category, as do Thailand and Malaysia, which appear to be following the path of export-driven growth. From the menu of services that the international accounting firms offer, it seems clear that all six export-oriented nations under consideration stand to gain from their involvement.

How such gains relate to domestic economic activities in the nations concerned varies considerably. As Hong Kong and Singapore are virtual city-states, there is little doubt that services offered locally by the firms and demonstration effects from their operations are strengthening their domestic economies. In the other four export-oriented nations, domestic impacts may be somewhat less visible. In Indonesia and the Philippines, the firms through their operations are providing some external linkage assistance to their clients. However, in those archipelagic nations the spread effects from their services may not have major impacts beyond Jakarta and Manila where they are concentrated. Even in those two rather large metropolitan complexes, the impact of the firms may have limited visibility because of the sheer size of the cities in question.

In the case of Thailand, the concentration of the firms in Bangkok may limit their impacts in the nation at large. Where the firms are in operation in the island economies of the Pacific, they can certainly contribute to strengthening essential international linkages. The smallness of the economies in question may insure more visible domestic impacts from the firms relative to what is occurring in the larger nations that have been discussed in this volume.

It cannot be said that the international accounting firms are central to the economic potential of the nations that have been discussed. However, they do provide various services that, together with the offerings of various other service subsectors, support a strengthening of external linkages and in some cases strengthen operations in domestic economies. Where the firms are offering a wide range of consulting services, they are certainly expanding their roles as facilitators. By providing local information to foreign interests, they are increasing the possibility of multinational firms locating facilities in the jurisdictions in question.

It seems clear that government policy makers should keep abreast of the potential that the firms have for impacting their economies. In cases where government agencies avail themselves of services offered by the firms, direct developmental impacts may result. The firms may have much to offer government agencies concerning the mechanics of international linkage. Nations where government agencies utilize the expertise available through the firms may attain certain developmental advantages. It seems clear that the governments concerned will do well to avail themselves of what the firms have to offer that may contribute to their goals. Despite the fact that the arrival of the firms is generally precipitated by their efforts to provide for the needs of their private-sector clients, the potential held by these firms for positive impacts to the public sector may become increasingly important.

# 12

## SOME FINAL REFLECTIONS

It seems clear that accounting services are important to economies enjoying various levels of development. Certainly they are important throughout the three groupings of economies highlighted in this volume. It is also clear that accounting services expand in volume as well as in diversity, reflecting the needs of business clients. They may also expand in response to legal dictates put forward by governments. Another source of their expansion may be the servicing of the needs of government and quasi-public agencies.

Accounting functions may also grow and diversify internal to corporate structures, although this circumstance has not been the concern of the present volume. As indicated in Chapter 3, the development of accounting services, whether internal to organizations or public, tends to parallel economic expansion. Accounting systems have emerged on a nation-specific basis, tailored to the needs of particular jurisdictions. It seems hardly surprising that accounting procedures and standards tend to reflect cultural, legal, political and economic environments, not to mention ways of doing business in each jurisdiction or region.

Such variations should presumably service the domestic needs of individual jurisdictions. How well they accommodate the needs of activities that are international in scope remains to be seen. Reporting systems and operating procedures used by accountants may tailor the information that they generate to national or regional requirements and characteristics. Corporations operating internationally may have to deal with these circumstances as their business takes them to various destinations.

As suggested in Chapter 3, accounting and reporting standards vary and must be treated differently depending upon the differing natures of economic and business climates in nations hosting components of multinational corporations. As economies expand, two aspects of accounting reporting must be considered. One concern relates to who controls the authority to set accounting and reporting standards. The other speaks to the effects of varying economic conditions and differing business arrangements on the hows and whys of accounting and reporting procedures. Domestic accounting services offered in various jurisdictions may present a heavy layer of complications for large firms operating in the international economy. A market for internationally based accounting services exists, and it is the strength of that market that has brought the major accounting firms into play in the jurisdictions highlighted in the present volume.

Traditionally, accounting standards have been the exclusive preserve of individual nations, which either established them through governmental agencies or commissioned professional accounting associations to perform that function. As far back as 1973 a group of national standard setters formed the International Accounting Standards Committee for the purpose of improving harmonization of national accounting standards. Although some progress has been made since that date, as emphasized in Chapter 3, there is still no single global system by which public accounting and financial reporting is accomplished in all parts of the world, and accounting systems remain largely nation-state specific. Although it has been demonstrated in the present volume that the nations of the Pacific have rather elaborate domestic legal and accounting systems in place, important roles for the major accounting firms seem obvious. Because the nations in question are dependent upon foreign linkages for their economic health, the international accounting firms have much to contribute as facilitators.

Certainly domestic laws and regulations can do a great deal toward providing stable predictable business climates conducive to the health of the economies in which they operate. Such institutional arrangements and the accountants and other practitioners who reinforce them are necessary to the success of their respective jurisdictions. If success requires strong linkages to the international economy, the domestic institutional arrangements and the accountants to support them may not be sufficient to support a successful economy. Of course, in some circumstances institutional arrangements may be inadequate and thus not supportive of economic expansion. Domestic arrangements and personnel may actually retard international linkages in some cases. In such circumstances the international accounting firms may have significant contributions to make.

Among the three groups of nations discussed in this volume, it is apparent that accounting practices are both defined and controlled by combinations of public and private prescriptive agencies. All of the jurisdictions alluded to have laws governing the specifics of the operations of business firms and what financial documents firms must provide to demonstrate that they are following the rules. In some cases the laws in question are modeled after those of various developed nations. Many of the economies that were discussed either are or have been governed or controlled by Great Britain. Thus their legal frameworks bear some likeness to the laws of that nation. United States influence is apparent in the Philippines, while that of the Dutch can be seen in Indonesia. Despite such resemblances, most of the jurisdictions concerned have developed certain laws and operating procedures reflecting the needs of their domestic economies.

In general, the jurisdictions that have been the concern of the present volume have organizations or government agencies that prescribe what one must accomplish in order to be considered to be a professional accountant. Various specifics differ from one jurisdiction to another, but in all cases entry into the accounting profession is carefully controlled. This of course insures that business firms retaining the services of accountants can rely on a certain level of expertise. In some of the larger or more developed nations, the ranks of the accounting profession are considerable.

In most cases the reason for the emergence of the major international accounting firms in specific jurisdictions has not been a shortage of practitioners. Thailand appears to be the only jurisdiction alluded to where a definite shortage of accountants exists. Numbers of accountants may not be a reliable measure for the impact of the profession in specific jurisdictions. As suggested in Chapter 10, a better understanding may be gained by examining the size of the profession against what the laws of the land expect from it. In most cases alluded to in this volume, the major accounting firms have emerged with the intent of servicing the needs of their international clients rather than to fill an obvious void occasioned by a shortfall of local accountants.

As suggested in Chapter 10, with the emergence of the global economy, international linkages and operations have become crucial elements in the development potential and material strength of the jurisdictions under consideration. This has increased the potential importance of the major international accounting firms. Certainly, domestic laws and procedures have established the ground rules for business and economic activity within the jurisdictions under consideration. Those laws and procedures also impact international linkages and business operations. Indeed, the compatibility of domestic laws and arrangements with the functioning of international business interests may encourage or retard such operations. In such circumstances the major international accounting firms may have much to offer.

Certainly, various business services, including the offerings of the major accounting firms, are capable of influencing the business climate in jurisdictions of all sizes and levels of development. However, the intensity of such influences can vary widely from place to place. Nations that rely heavily upon exports to fuel their economies will have definite and perhaps increasing needs with respect to services that facilitate international business operations. How influential such services and the firms that provide them may be in specific economies may depend upon the size and sophistication of the domestic components of those economies, the availability and skill of local accountants and of course the size and nature of export sectors.

It seems clear that the international accounting firms have much to offer to the newly industrialized nations discussed in this volume. All of those nations have definite needs relating to the support and encouragement of their international sectors. The same can be said of Thailand and Malaysia, which have also elected export-driven growth strategies. Certainly these last two nations, together with the "Asian Tigers," stand to benefit from the menu of services being offered by the international accounting firms.

As mentioned in Chapter 11, how such benefits relate to domestic economic activities in the nations concerned varies considerably. Hong Kong and Singapore, as virtual city-states, may benefit from demonstration effects from the activities of the major accounting firms, although both of the jurisdictions in question have sizeable cohorts of indigenous accountants. In South Korea, Taiwan and Thailand, domestic impacts from the firms may be somewhat less visible. In Malaysia, where the firms have penetrated regional centers, there may be more potential for domestic impacts.

As archipelagic nations, Indonesia and the Philippines may not be enjoying spread effects from services provided by the firms beyond Jakarta and Manila where they are concentrated. However, the firms through their operations are providing some external linkages for their clients. As suggested in Chapter 11, the impacts of the firms in Jakarta and Manila may have limited visibility because of the size of the cities in question.

Among the small island economies of the Pacific, the firms may have more noticeable impacts. While assisting with external linkages, they may also provide visible domestic impacts. Indeed, domestic impacts may be relatively more intense the smaller the jurisdictions concerned. Even among the small island economies it cannot be presumed that the firms are a central feature of their economic potential.

In the national groupings discussed in this volume, the firms do provide various services that, together with various other service subsectors, assist in the strengthening of external linkages. In some cases they may be instrumental in strengthening aspects of their host economies as well.

In most of the economies in question the firms are offering a wide and perhaps expanding range of consulting services. Through these offerings they are not only expanding their roles as facilitators, they are also expanding their potential for impacting wide ranges of endeavors within the domestic preserves of their host economies. Additionally, as suggested in Chapter 11, by providing local information to foreign interests they are increasing the possibility of multinational firms locating facilities in the jurisdictions in question.

Through their consulting activities it is possible that the firms may find various government agencies among their clients. Where that occurs, it seems obvious that the firms have the opportunity to impact economies directly. The firms have much to offer governmental agencies concerning operations in the world economy. Despite the fact that the firms have arrived in most of the jurisdictions discussed in this volume in response to the needs of private clients, governmental contracts have the potential for considerable expansion.

In a relative sense the potential impacts of the firms may be greater in smaller and poorer jurisdictions. This is not to suggest that their impact in larger, more developed jurisdictions may be unimportant. In those jurisdictions the domestic economy may be large enough and sufficiently staffed by accountants and other providers of sophisticated business services to prevent the work of the firms from standing out. Nonetheless, what the firms are doing throughout the economies discussed here provides an excellent example of the facilitative role of multinational service firms in the world economy.

# SELECTED BIBLIOGRAPHY

Abu Amara, Yosra. 1991. *Selected International Trade in Services and Development in Small Island Economies*. Ph.D. diss. Kent State University.

Akathaporn, Parporn, Adel M. Novin, and Mohammad J. Abdolmohammadi. 1993. "Accounting Education and Practice in Thailand: Perceived Problems and Effectiveness of Enhancement Strategies." *International Journal of Accounting* 28 (3): 259–272.

Alam, M. Shahid. 1989. *Governments and Markets in Economic Development Strategies: Lessons from Korea, Taiwan and Japan*. New York: Praeger.

Amara, Yosra A. 1993a. "Externally Traded Services and the Development of Small Economies." In *External Linkages and Growth in Small Economies*, edited by David L. McKee, 7–14. Westport, Conn.: Praeger.

———. 1993b. "Services and Growth in Small Developing Countries." In *External Linkages and Growth in Small Economies*, edited by David L. McKee, 17–26. Westport, Conn.: Praeger.

American Institute of Certified Public Accountants. 1965. *Accounting Research Study No. 7, Inventory of Generally Accepted Accounting Principles for Business Enterprises*. New York: American Institute of Certified Public Accountants.

———. 1991. *International Accounting and Auditing Standards*. New York: American Institute of Certified Public Accountants.

Amsden, Alice H. 1989. *Asia's Next Giant: South Korea and Late Industrialization*. New York: Oxford University Press.

Ariff, Mohamed. 1991. *The Malaysian Economy: Pacific Connections*. New York: Oxford University Press.

Ariff, Mohamed, and Hal Hill. 1985. *Export-oriented Industrialisation: The ASEAN Experience*. Boston: Allen and Unwin.

Balassa, Bela, and John Williamson. 1990. *Adjusting to Success: Balance of Payments Policy in the East Asian NIC's*. 2d ed. Washington, D.C.: Institute for International Economics.

Bavishi, Vinod. 1991. *International Accounting and Auditing Trends*. 2d ed. Princeton, N.J.: Center for International Analysis and Research.

Bello, Walden F. 1982. *Development Debacle: The World Bank in the Philippines*. San Francisco, Calif.: Institute for Food and Development Policy.

Bertram, I. G., and R. F. Watters. 1985. "The MIRAB Economy in South Pacific Microstates." *Pacific Viewpoint* 26 (3): 497–519.

————. 1986. "The MIRAB Process: Some Earlier Analysis in Context." *Pacific Viewpoint* 27 (1): 47–59.

Birenbaum, D. E., and S. Rosenblatt. 1985. "Trade Trends and Trade Issues in the Pacific Basin." *Philippine Economic Journal* 24 (4): 288–301.

Bosworth, S. W. 1992. "The United States and Asia." *Foreign Affairs* 71 (1): 113–129.

Boyce, J. K. 1992. "The Revolving Door? External Debts and Capital Flight: A Philippine Case Study." *World Development* 20 (3): 335–349.

Bradford, Colin I., Jr., and William H. Branson. 1987. *Trade and Structural Change in Pacific Asia*. National Bureau of Economic Research Conference Report Series. Chicago and London: University of Chicago Press, 1987.

Browne, Christopher, with Douglas A. Scott. 1989. *Economic Development in Seven Pacific Island Countries*. Washington, D.C.: International Monetary Fund.

Buckley, Peter J., and Jeremy Clegg, eds. 1991. *Multinational Enterprises in Less Developed Countries*. New York: St. Martin's Press.

Byrne and Co. 1988. *The Accounting Profession in Hong Kong*. New York: American Institute of Certified Public Accountants.

Castle, Leslie, and Christopher Findlay, eds. 1988. *Pacific Trade in Services*. Sydney: Allen and Unwin.

Chan, P. K. L., and J. H. Y. Wong. 1985. "The Effect of Exchange Rate Variability on Hong Kong's Exports." *Hong Kong Economic Papers* 16: 27–39.

Chen, E. K. Y. 1984. "Exports of Technology by Newly Industrialized Countries: Hong Kong." *World Development* 12 (5/6): 481–490.

Cheng, C. Y. 1985. "Economic Development on Both Sides of the Taiwan Straits: New Trends for Convergence." *Hong Kong Economic Papers* 16: 54–73.

Chew, Soon Beng. 1988. *Small Firms in Singapore*. New York: Oxford University Press. For the National University of Singapore, Faculty of Arts and Social Sciences, Center for Advanced Studies.

Cho, George. 1990. *The Malaysian Economy: Spatial Perspectives*. London: Routledge.

Chow, P. C. Y. 1990. "Output Effect, Technology Change and Labor Absorption in Taiwan, 1952–1986." *Economic Development and Cultural Change* 39 (1): 77–88.

Chowdhury, A., and C. H. Kirkpatrick. 1990. "Human Resources, Factor Intensity and Comparative Advantage of ASEAN." *Journal of Economic Studies* 17: 14–26.

Cole, R. V., and T. G. Parry. 1986. *Selected Issues in Pacific Island Development: Papers from the Islands/Australia Project*. Pacific Policy Papers Series, No. 2. Canberra: Australian National University, National Center for Development Studies.

Collins, Stephen H. 1989. "The Move to Globalization: An Interview with Ralph E. Walters." *Journal of Accountancy* 167 (3): 82–85.

Cooper, Richard. 1988. "Survey of Issues and Review." In *Pacific Trade in Services*, edited by Leslie Castle and Christopher Findlay, 247–262. Sydney: Allen and Unwin.

Coopers and Lybrand. 1991. *International Accounting Summaries*. New York: John Wiley and Sons.

————. 1992. *International Accounting Summaries 1992 Supplement*. New York: John Wiley and Sons.

*CPA Journal*. 1992. "International Accounting Standards: Are They Coming to America?" *CPA Journal* 62 (10) 16–18, 21–24.

Cragg, Claudia. 1993. *Hunting with the Tigers: Doing Business with Hong Kong, Indonesia, South Korea, Malaysia, the Philippines, Singapore, Taiwan, Thailand and Vietnam*. San Diego: Pfeiffer and Company.

David Tong and Company. 1993. *The Accounting Profession in Singapore*. New York: American Institute of Certified Public Accountants.

*The Economist*. 1989. "A Survey of Hong Kong: Weighing the Odds." June.

————. 1993. "A Survey of Indonesia: Wealth in Its Grasp." April 17, p. 3.

*The Economist* Supplement. 1991. "A Survey of Asia's Emerging Economies: Where Tigers Breed." November 16.

Elegant, Robert. 1990. *Pacific Destiny: Inside Asia Today*. New York: Crown Publishers.

Enderwick, Peter, ed. 1989. *Multinational Service Firms*. New York: Routledge.

————. 1991. "Service Sector Multinationals and Developing Countries." In *Multinational Enterprises in Less Developed Countries*, edited by Peter J. Buckley and Jeremy Clegg, 292–309. New York: St. Martin's Press.

Ernst and Young. 1990. *Doing Business in Thailand*. New York: Ernst and Young International.

Estanislao, J. P. 1984. "A Perspective on Our Economic Crisis." *Philippine Economic Journal* 23 (1): 12–22.

Euh, Yoon-Dae, and James C. Baker. 1990. *The Korean Banking System and Foreign Influence*. London and New York: Routledge.

Fairbairn, T'eo. 1985. "Economic Prospects for the Pacific Islands." In *The Pacific Islands in the Year 2000*, edited by Kiste, Robert C., and Richard A. Herr, 44–69. Manoa: Working Paper Series, Pacific Islands Study Program, Center for Asian and Pacific Studies, University of Hawaii. In collaboration with the Pacific Islands Development Program, East-West Center, Honolulu.

Fairbairn, T'eo, I. J. Thomas, and T. G. Parry. 1986. *Multinational Enterprises in the Developing South Pacific Region.* Honolulu: East-West Center.

Feketekuty, Geza. 1988. *International Trade in Services.* Cambridge: Ballinger Publishing Company.

Gardner, Paul F. 1989. *New Enterprise in the South Pacific: The Indonesian and Melanesian Experience.* Washington, D.C.: National Defense University Press.

Grone, Donald K. 1983. *The ASEAN States: Coping with Dependence.* New York: Praeger.

Gullick, J. M. 1981. *Malaysia: Economic Expansion and National Unity.* Boulder, Colo.: Westview Press.

Hakchung, C. 1989. "The Asian Newly Industrializing Economies (NIES): Are Economic Miracles Equally Miraculous?" *Singapore Economic Review* 34 (1): 2–12.

Hamilton, Clive, and Richard Tanter. 1987. "The Antinomies of Success in South Korea." *Journal of International Affairs* 41 (1): 63–90.

Heely, James A., and Roy L Nersesian. 1993. *Global Management Accounting: A Guide for Executives of International Corporations.* Westport, Conn.: Quorum Books.

Heng, T. M., and L. Lon. 1990. "An Asian NIC's View on Service Trade Liberalization: Singapore's Case." *Journal of Economic Development* (December): 57–82.

Holmes, Sir Frank, ed. 1987. *Economic Adjustment: Policies and Problems.* Washington, D.C. International Monetary Fund.

Igbal, B. A., and S. U. Faroogi. 1985. "Taiwan's Trade: Problem of Plenty." *Journal of World Trade Law* 19 (6): 673–674.

International Accounting Standards Committee. 1990. *International Accounting Standards.* Reprinted in American Institute of Certified Public Accountants. 1991. *International Accounting and Auditing Standards.* Chicago: Commerce Clearing House.

Islam, I., and C. Kirkpatrick. 1986. "Export-Led Development, Labour-Market Conditions and the Distribution of Income: The Case of Singapore." *Cambridge Journal of Economics* 10 (2): 113–127.

Jansen, Karel. 1990. *Finance, Growth and Stability: Financing Economic Development in Thailand, 1960–1986.* Sydney: Gower, Avebury.

Jomo, Kwame Sumdaram. 1990. *Growth and Structural Change in the Malaysian Economy.* New York: St. Martin's Press.

*Journal of Accountancy.* 1989. "IASC Study Confirms Use of International Standards." *Journal of Accountancy* 167 (3): 85.

————. 1994. "IASC Completes Comparability Project, Receives IOSCO Endorsement." *Journal of Accountancy* 177 (1): 23.

Kelly, Brian, and Mark London. 1989. *The Four Little Dragons*. New York: Simon and Schuster.

Kim, Chungsoo, and Kihong Kim. 1990. "Asian NIE's and Liberalization of Trade in Services." In *Pacific Initatives in Global Trade*, edited by H. E. English, 181–198. Vancouver: Institute for Research on Public Policy.

Kim, Kihwan. 1988. "Korea in the 1990s: Making the Transition to a Developed Economy." *World Development* 16 (1): 7–18.

Kim, W. C., and A. E. Tschoegl. 1986. "The Regional Balance of Industrialization: An Empirical Investigation of the Asian Pacific Area." *Journal of Developing Areas* 20 (2): 173–183.

KPMG San Tong and Co. 1990. *The Accounting Profession in South Korea*. New York: American Institute of Certified Public Accountants.

Kraus, Willy, and Wilfried Lutkenhorst. 1986. *The Economic Development of the Pacific Basin: Growth Dynamics, Trade Relations and Emerging Cooperation*. New York: St. Martin's Press; London: Hurst.

Krause, L. B. 1988. "Hong Kong and Singapore: Twins or Kissing Cousins?" *Economic Development and Cultural Change* 36 (3, supplement): S45–66.

Kulessa, Manfred. 1990. *The Newly Industrializing Economies of Asia: Prospects of Co-operation*. Europe-Asia-Pacific Studies in Economy and Technology. New York: Springer.

Lav, Lawrence J. 1986. *Models of Development: A Comparative Study of Economic Growth in South Korea and Taiwan*. San Francisco: Institute of Contemporary Studies Press.

Lee, C. H. 1992. "The Government, Financial System and Large Private Enterprises in the Economic Development of South Korea." *World Development* 20 (2): 187–197.

Lee, Chung H., and Ippei Yamazawa. 1990. *The Economic Development of Japan and Korea: A Parallel with Lessons*. New York: Praeger.

Li, Kuo-Ting. 1988. *The Evolution of Policy behind Taiwan's Development Success*. New Haven: Yale University Press.

Lim, Chong Yah, et al. 1989. *Policy Options for the Singapore Economy*. New York: McGraw-Hill.

Lim, David. 1985. *Asian-Australia Trade in Manufacturers*. Melbourne: Longman Cheshire.

Lim, Patricia. 1984. *ASEAN: A Bibliography*. Singapore: Institute of Southeast Asian Studies.

Linder, S. B. 1985. "Pacific Protagonist: Implications of the Rising Role of the Pacific." *American Economic Review* 75 (2): 279–284.

Linder, Staffan Burenstam. 1986. *The Pacific Century: Economic and Political Consequences of Asian-Pacific Dynamism*. Stanford, Calif.: Stanford University Press.

Livingstone, John M. 1990. "Accounting Standards and Practices." *Management Accounting* 72 (2): 33. Reprinted from John M. Livingston, *Internationalization of Business*. New York: St. Martin's Press.

McKee, David L. 1988. *Growth, Development and the Service Economy in the Third World*. New York: Praeger.

————. 1991. *Schumpeter and the Political Economy of Change*. New York: Praeger.

McKee, David L., and Don E. Garner. 1992. *Accounting Services: The International Economy and Third World Development*. Westport, Conn.: Praeger.

McKee, David L., and Clem Tisdell. 1990. *Developmental Issues in Small Island Economies*. New York: Praeger.

McKee, David L., Xiannuan Lin, and Haiyang Chen. 1991. "Hong Kong's Investment in China and the Hong Kong Economy." *Philippine Economic Journal* xxx (3&4): 224–236.

McLellan, S. 1985. "Malaysia's New Economic Policy: The Role of the Transnational Corporations." *Canadian Journal of Development Studies* 6 (1): 65–75.

Martin, Linda G. 1987. *The ASEAN Success Story: Social, Economic, and Political Dimensions*. Honolulu: East-West Center, University of Hawaii Press.

Meller, Norman. 1987. "The Pacific Island Microstates." *Journal of International Affairs* 41 (1): 109–134.

Metraux, Daniel Alfred. 1991. *Taiwan's Political and Economic Growth in the Late 20th Century*. Lewiston, N.Y.: E. Mellen Press.

Mody, A. 1990. "Institutions and Dynamic Comparative Advantage: The Electronics Industry in South Korea and Taiwan." *Cambridge Journal of Economics* 14 (3): 291–314.

Morrison, Charles Edward. 1985. *Japan, the United States, and a Changing Southeast Asia*. Lanham, Md.: University Press of America.

Most, Kenneth S. 1988. *Advances in International Accounting*. Vol. 2. *A Research Annual*. Greenwich, Conn.: JAI Press.

Mueller, Gerhard G., Helen Gernon, and Gary Meek. 1991. *Accounting: An International Perspective*. 2d ed. Homewood, Ill.: Richard D. Irwin.

Nobes, Christopher, and Robert Parker, eds. 1991. *Comparative International Accounting*. 3d ed., New York: Prentice-Hall.

Noland, Marcus. 1990. *Pacific Basin Developing Countries*. Washington, D.C.: Institute for International Economies.

Noyelle, Thierry J., and Anna B. Dutka. 1988. *International Trade in Business Services*. Cambridge: Ballinger Publishing Company.

Nurkse, Ragnar. 1967. *Problems of Capital Formation in Underdeveloped Countries and Patterns of Trade and Development*. New York: Oxford University Press.

O'Malley, Shaun F. 1992. "Accounting across Borders." *Financial Executive* 8 (2): 28–31.

Orsini, Larry L., and Lawrence R. Hudack. 1992. "EEC Financial Reporting: Another Source of Harmonization of Accounting Principles." *CPA Journal* 62 (10): 20.

Paauw, D. S. 1984. "Economic Growth, Employment, and Productivity: Prospects for Indonesia." *Singapore Economic Review* 29 (2): 111–125.

Palmer, Ronald D., and Thomas J. Reckford. 1987. *Building ASEAN: 20 Years of Southeast Asian Cooperation*. New York: Praeger.

Park, Y. C. 1986. "Foreign Debt, Balance of Payments, and Growth Prospects: The Case of the Republic of Korea, 1965-1988." *World Development* 14 (8): 1019–1058.

Parry, T. G. 1988. "Foreign Investment and Industry in the Pacific Islands." *Journal of Developing Areas* 22 (3): 381–399.

Parry, Thomas G. 1973. "The International Firm and National Economic Policy." *Economic Journal* 84 (332): 84–88.

Peavey, Dennis E., and Stuart K. Webster. 1990. "Is GAAP the Gap to International Markets?" *Management Accounting* 72 (2): 31–35.

Peebles, Gavin. 1988. *Hong Kong's Economy: An Introductory Macro Economic Analysis*. New York: Oxford University Press.

Perroux, Francois. 1950. "Economic Space: Theory and Applications." *Quarterly Journal of Economics* 64 (1): 90–97.

———. 1970. "Note on Concept of Growth Poles." In *Regional Economics*, edited by David L. McKee, Robert D. Dean and William H. Leahy, 93–104. New York: Free Press.

Price Waterhouse. 1989a. *Doing Business in Fiji*. New York: Price Waterhouse World Firm Limited.

———. 1989b. *Doing Business in Indonesia*. New York: Price Waterhouse World Firm Limited.

———. 1989c. *Doing Business in the Philippines*. New York: Price Waterhouse World Firm Limited.

———. 1990a. *Doing Business in Malayasia*. New York: Price Waterhouse World Firm Limited.

———. 1990b. *Doing Business in Papua New Guinea*. New York: Price Waterhouse World Firm Limited.

———. 1990c. *Doing Business in Singapore*. New York: Price Waterhouse World Firm Limited.

———. 1991a. *Doing Business in Taiwan*. New York: Price Waterhouse World Firm Limited.

———. 1991b. *Doing Business in Western Samoa*. New York: Price Waterhouse World Firm Limited.

———. 1992a. *Doing Business in Hong Kong*. New York: Price Waterhouse World Firm Limited.

————. 1992b. *Doing Business in Korea.* New York: Price Waterhouse World Firm Limited.

————. 1992c. *Doing Business in Malaysia: Supplement.* New York: Price Waterhouse World Firm Limited.

————. 1992d. *Doing Business in Vanuatu.* New York: Price Waterhouse World Firm Limited.

————. 1993a. *Doing Business in Indonesia.* New York: Price Waterhouse World Firm Limited.

————. 1993b. *Doing Business in the Philippines.* New York: Price Waterhouse World Firm Limited.

————. 1993c. *Doing Business in Singapore.* New York: Price Waterhouse World Firm Limited.

————. 1994a. *Doing Business in Fiji.* New York: Price Waterhouse World Firm Limited.

————. 1994b. *Doing Business in Malaysia.* New York: Price Waterhouse World Firm Limited.

Rabushka, Alvin. 1987. *The New China: Comparative Economic Development in Mainland China, Taiwan, and Hong Kong.* Boulder, Colo.: Westview Press.

Rahmon, M. Z. and J. E. Finnerty. 1986. "International Accounting Standards and Transnational Corporations." *Revista Internationale di Scienze Economiche e Commercial* 33 (No. 6–7): 697–714.

Rana, P. B., and J. M. Dowling, Jr. 1988. "The Impact of Foreign Capital on Growth: Evidence from Asian Developing Countries." *Developing Economics* 26 (1): 3–11.

Rhee, Yung Whee, Bruce Ross-Larson, and Garry Pursell. 1984. *Korea's Competitive Edge: Managing the Entry into World Markets.* Baltimore: Johns Hopkins University Press.

Riahi-Belkaoui, Ahmed. 1994. *Accounting in the Developing Countries.* Westport, Conn.: Quorum Books.

Sassen, Saskia. 1991. *The Global City: New York, London, Tokyo.* Princeton: Princeton University Press.

Schive, C., and B. A. Majumdar. 1990. "Direct Foreign Investment and Linkage Effects: The Experience of Taiwan." *Canadian Journal of Development Studies* 11 (2): 325–342.

Schlosstein, Steven. 1991. *Asia's New Little Dragons.* Chicago: Contemporary Books.

SGV and Co. and Arthur Andersen and Co. 1989. *The Accounting Profession in the Philippines.* New York: American Institute of Certified Public Accountants.

Siamwalla, A. 1990. "The Thai Rural Credit System: Public Subsidies, Private Information, and Segmented Markets." *World Bank Economic Review* 4 (3) 271–295.

Skully, Michael T. 1985. *ASEAN Financial Co-operation: Developments in Banking, Finance, and Insurance*. New York: St. Martin's Press.

Skully, Michael T., and George J. Viksnins. 1987. *Financing East Asia's Success: Comparative Financial Development in Eight Asian Countries*. New York: St. Martin's Press.

Smith, Bruce J. 1987. "Some Aspects of Economic Adjustment in Small Island Economies." In *Economic Adjustment: Policies and Problems*, Sir Frank Holmes (ed.). Washington, D.C. International Monetary Fund.

Soong, T. N., and Co. 1992. *The Accounting Profession in Taiwan, Republic of China*. New York: American Institute of Certified Public Accountants.

Streeten, Paul. 1988. *Beyond Adjustment: The Asian Experience*. Washington, D.C.: International Monetary Fund.

Suarez-Villa, L., and P. H. Han. 1990. "The Rise of Korea's Electronics Industry: Technological Change, Growth, and Territorial Distribution." *Economic Geography* 66 (3): 273–292.

Sudit, E. F. 1984. "The Role of Comparative Productivity Accounting in Export Decisions." *Journal of International Business Studies* 15 (1): 105–118.

Sundrum, R. M. 1986. "Indonesia's Rapid Economic Growth, 1968–1981." *Bulletin of Indonesian Economic Studies* 22 (3): 40–69.

Sung, Yun Wing. 1988. "A Theoretical and Empirical Analysis of Entrepôt Trade: Hong Kong and Singapore and Their Roles in China's Trade." In *Pacific Trade in Services*, edited by Leslie Castle and Christopher Findlay, 173–208. Sydney: Allen and Unwin.

Sutherland, W. M. 1986. "Microstates and Unequal Trade in the South Pacific: The Sparteca Agreement of 1980." *Journal of World Trade Law* 20 (3): 313–328.

Thoburn, John T. 1977. *Primary Commodity Exports and Economic Development: Theory, Evidence and a Study of Malaysia*. London and New York: Wiley.

Tisdell, Clem. 1993. "Small Island Economies in a World of Economic Change." Mimeograph. University of Queensland.

Todaro, Michael P. 1994. *Economic Development*. 5th ed., New York: Longman.

Tucker, Ken, and Mark Sundberg. 1988. *International Trade in Services*. London: Routledge.

United Nations. 1987. *Foreign Direct Investment, the Service Sector and International Banking*. New York: United Nations Center on Transnational Corporations.

Valentine, Charles F., Ginger Lew, and Roger M. Poor. 1991. *The Ernst & Young Resource Guide to Global Markets*. New York: Wiley.

Vogel, Ezra F. 1991. *The Four Little Dragons: The Spread of Industrialization in East Asia*. Cambridge, Mass.: Harvard University Press.

Wallace, R. S. Olusegun, John M. Samuels, and Richard J. Briston. 1990. *Research in Third World Accounting*, vol. 1. London: JAI Press Ltd.

Walter, Ingo. 1990. *The Secret Money Market*. New York: Harper and Row Publishers, Ballinger Division.

Wawn, Brian. 1982. *The Economies of the ASEAN Countries: Indonesia, Malaysia, Philippines, Singapore, and Thailand*. New York: St. Martin's Press.

Westphal, L. E. 1990. "Industrial Policy in an Export-Propelled Economy: Lessons from South Korea's Experience." *Journal of Economic Perspectives* 4 (3): 41–59.

————, et al. 1984. "Exports of Technology by Newly Industrializing Countries: Republic of Korea." *World Development* 12 (5/6): 505–533.

Wie, T. K. 1991. "The Surge of Asian NIC Investment into Indonesia." *Bulletin of Indonesian Economic Studies* 27 (3): 55–88.

World Bank. 1992. *World Development Report*. New York: Oxford University Press.

Wyatt, Arthur R. 1992. "Seeking Credibility in a Global Economy." *New Accountant* 8 (1): 4–6, 51, 52.

Yamazawa, Il, T. Nohera, and H. Osada. 1986. "Economic Interdependence in Pacific Asia: An International Input-Output Analysis." *Development Economics* 24 (2): 95–108.

# INDEX

accountants, 48, 50, 57, 59, 60, 64, 67, 69, 100, 125, 131, 135, 137, 155, 157–59

Accountants Registration Board of Papua New Guinea, 75, 135

accounting, 4, 28, 33, 41, 43, 49, 58, 63, 90, 98, 114, 119, 124, 135, 147; education, 28, 126; firms, 5, 85, 87, 88; information, 27, 28, 34, 35; methods, 27, 47, 52, 109, 123; organizations, 27, 56; practitioners, 27, 28, 45, 120, 122, 124, 135, 137; procedures, 32–34, 41, 45–47, 60, 61, 63, 71, 120, 126, 129, 136, 137, 155, 157; reports, 28, 30, 31, 36, 62, 68, 75, 113, 156; requirements, 29, 30, 31, 32, 36, 49, 50, 73, 124; services, 5, 35–37, 49, 60, 85–88, 95–97, 108, 109, 111, 115, 137, 139, 143, 145, 150, 155; standards, 34, 43, 52, 57, 59, 64, 69, 73, 75, 120, 126–28, 131–34, 136, 150, 156; systems, 27, 29, 30–33, 35–37, 87, 98, 113, 155

Accounting Research and Development Foundation, 45, 46, 122

Accounting Standards Advisory Board, 43, 120

advances: in communications, 103, 106; in transportation, 103, 104, 106

Africa, 16

agriculture, 7, 19, 22, 92, 94, 105, 144

American Institute of Certified Public Accountants, 37, 61, 129

American Samoa, 113

annual report, 48, 97

appraisal, 50, 58, 125

ASEAN, 79, 80, 92

Asia, 15, 16, 22, 24, 25, 84, 91

Asian nations, 8, 23, 26, 80, 140

Asian Tigers, 8, 24, 25, 67, 79, 95, 145, 158

Asia/Pacific region, 84, 86, 92, 93, 95

assets, 42, 43, 46, 47, 50, 52, 61, 62, 69

audit, 48, 51, 60, 63, 68, 75, 113, 114, 120, 124; functions, 36, 57, 85, 109, 110, 128; requirements, 29, 37, 42, 49, 50, 72, 124, 134;

## About the Authors

DON E. GARNER is professor and chair of the department of accounting at California State University, Stanislaus. He is a certified public accountant and a certified internal auditor as well as a specialist in auditing and accounting theory. His research has appeared in various professional publications, including *Accounting Review*, *Journal of Accountancy*, *The Internal Auditor*, and *Government Accountants Journal*.

DAVID L. McKEE is professor of economics at Kent State University where he is a specialist in economic development and regional economics. His recent books include *Urban Environments in Emerging Economies*; *Energy, the Environment and Public Policy: Issues for the 1990's* (edited); *Schumpeter and the Political Economy of Change*; *Growth, Development, and the Service Economy in the Third World*; and *Developmental Issues in Small Island Economies* (coauthored with Clement Tisdell), all published by Praeger.

Together the authors have published *Accounting Services, the International Economy, and Third World Development* (Praeger, 1992).

ISBN 1-56720-017-6

HARDCOVER BAR CODE

# DATE DUE

| | | | |
|---|---|---|---|
| | | | |
| | | | |
| | | | |
| | | | |
| | | | |
| | | | |
| | | | |
| | | | |
| | | | |
| | | | |
| | | | |
| | | | |
| | | | |
| | | | |
| | | | |
| | | | |

Demco, Inc. 38-293